PRACTICAL PERFORMANCE APPRAISAL

Practical Performance Appraisal

Designing, installing, and maintaining performance appraisal systems

VALERIE STEWART, BA PhD
ANDREW STEWART, MA PhD

Gower

First published 1977 by
Gower Press, Teakfield Limited

Reprinted 1979, 1980

Reprinted 1981, 1987 by Gower Publishing Company Limited, Croft Road, Aldershot, Hampshire GU11 3HR, England

British Library Cataloguing in Publication Data

Stewart, Valerie
   Practical performance appraisal.
   1. Employees, Rating of
   I. Title   II. Stewart, Andrew, b.1942
   658.31'25   HF5549.5.R3

   ISBN 0-566-02081-5

Typeset by Preface Ltd, Salisbury, Wilts
Printed and bound in Great Britain by
Biddles Ltd, Guildford and King's Lynn

Contents

List of figures   vi

Preface   vii

1   The benefits of performance appraisal   1

2   Appraisal systems in action   16

3   Installing a system: performance criteria   37

4   Installing a system: system design   60

5   Installing a system: training   79

6   Monitoring and control   97

7   Problem performers   121

8   Performance appraisal systems in context   136

9   Relations with outside bodies   155

10 Speculations on the future   164

References   176

Bibliography   179

Index   181

Figures

2.1   Appraisal form used by the A—Z Retailing
Company Ltd   18
2.2   Scales describing the attributes of the appraisee on
the appraisal form used by Cloud, Cuckoo &
Partners Ltd   22
2.3   The main variations in appraisal systems   34
3.1   Performance questionnaire with list of bipolar
statements   44
3.2   Pen pictures, derived from completed performance
questionnaires, showing the characteristics
associated with (a) an effective and (b) an
ineffective manager   45
4.1   Appraisal purposes and system design   61
Appendixes
6.1   Survey of management development systems   111
6.2   Managers' appraisal survey   118

Preface

Performance appraisal has been with us for some time now. Some firms are on their third or fourth re-design; others are contemplating whether an appraisal system would be useful at all. We hope to have something helpful to say to both parties, and to the people in between.

In this book we ask the reader to start with a blank sheet of paper, more or less, and to consider the issues he encounters when designing an appraisal system. For all the quantities of literature that have been compiled on appraisal systems, very little has started with this basic question: what kind of alterations do you want to make to your organisation with your appraisal system? Many appraisal systems which have foundered, have been lost because they were not designed with a clear set of purposes in mind. A personnel manager came from a firm that had a system into a firm that didn't, and pirated his old form; a consultant installed a standard system, complete with standard paperwork; a committee designed something, on the usual principles of committee decision-making. To assist the reader who wants firmer guidance, we devote a good deal of space in this book to methods of establishing performance criteria and to designing appraisal systems with a given purpose in mind.

Training for appraisal is treated in some detail; we have suffered at all points along the appraisal-training spectrum, and give some advice on training design which the committed trainer will be able to use. Another neglected area of appraisal systems has been the maintenance of a system once it is installed. A gardener worth his salt doesn't stick a plant in the ground, label it, and then forget it; he tends, feeds, and watches over it during its infancy, prunes and trims and shapes it when it matures, and pulls it out of the soil when it is over before it takes out nourishment that would be better left for its successor. However, many an appraisal system is planted in the organisation by the personnel department, who are then satisfied that they have an appraisal system – the paperwork tells them so. They ignore the early cries of management that might tell them how the system's settling down; later on, when the business has changed, the labour market has altered, and the system is out-of-date, they remain blindfold. Should the system deteriorate to the point where managers are using it for punishment, or for meeting their own political ends, they still do not see; so that any better-intentioned specialist who tries to remedy the situation finds the ground poisoned against appraisal systems for a long time. Care, maintenance, and research are needed, and we have some suggestions for doing this.

We also discuss the context within which appraisal happens. There are two sorts of context; one is the organisational context — how does the appraisal system relate to selection, training, manpower planning, assessment of potential? And the second context is that of social change; how will appraisal systems respond to new employment legislation, legislation on privacy, union pressure, pay restraint, government interference? To some of these questions we may have answers; to others, only speculations.

Our own interest in appraisal systems comes from a number of sources. We were both lucky enough to be employed by an organisation – IBM – where appraisal practice is well developed and where senior managers go out of their way to listen to employee comments about the organisation. Here we had some opportunities to do research and to encounter live appraisal problems in a firm where appraisal was taken for granted. Since those days we have worked in and with a large variety of organisations, mostly on work to do with the identification and development of management potential. Inevitably this has brought more and more contact with appraisal systems of all varieties, ages, and conditions. Indeed, one of the things that constantly amazes us is the huge variety of appraisal systems that exists within the UK. Fom time to time we have lectured and written about appraisals and appraisal training, and from the questions people ask, have learned even more. From this experience we have evolved a set of prejudices, which we would like to state here:

appraisal systems should be primarily a tool for line management to do their job better. Personnel may gather useful information on the way but the line must 'own' the system;

even though appraisal systems can look like tools for punishment and for salary planning, their best use is for development, and self-development for preference;

the appraisal system is an intervention in the organisation's

process. It needs planning and managing professionally, like any
other intervention.

We have tried not to let our prejudices have too great an
influence, and the reader who wants to design a sophisticated
punishment system will read all about it in Chapter Four.

A note on terminology. We have tried not to use too many
jargon words, especially ones like *aim, goal, target,* which have
deeply held idiosyncratic meaning for some organisations. For
the sake of stylistic variation, we have used *appraiser* and
appraisee, manager and *employee,* and *manager* and *man,*
interchangeably. We do not intend to imply, by the use of
manager and *employee,* that managers are not appraised.
Similarly we have used *he* and *his* throughout; struggling not to
use 'sexist' language is a little like putting panties on puppies,
drawing attention to what you want people to take for granted.
People who take these things to heart may be refreshed to
discover that the senior author is female.

We have to thank many people for their assistance during the
writing of this book. Dick Cooper, of Fisons, provided many
ideas on research and counselling. Trevor Grigg, of Commercial
Union, John Stenton, of Philips Electrical, and Tim Reeder
(then of Price Waterhouse, now with Cooper Brothers), have
discussed their unusual and successful approaches to
performance appraisal. Ron Lambert, of Booker Belmont,
showed us how good in-house research could be done. Brian
Shenton, of Noble Lowndes, provided many useful ideas on the
subject of counselling, by both precept and example. Ed
Moorby, of the Air Transport and Travel Industry Training
Board, has been a useful source of information and full of
practical advice in seminars; Pat Terry and Norman Venus, of
the Chemical and Allied Products Industry Training Board,
have also given us much food for thought, especially in the area
of appraisal systems as interventions in an organisation. To all of
them, and to the many more who cannot be identified, we offer
our thanks.

To the reader who has borne with us to the end of this preface,
may we say that whether he wants to design a new system or re-
examine an old one, and whether he workds in a major multi-
national or in a small family firm, we hope he finds something
useful in this book. Appraisal systems are time-consuming and
thought-provoking, puzzling and rewarding; but in the right

hands they make the organisation a better and more efficient place to work.

Valerie Stewart
Andrew Stewart
July 1977

1 The benefits of performance appraisal

'If you don't know where you're going, you'll most likely end up somewhere else.' Thus Dr Peter, of 'Peter Principle' fame, pointing out the importance of planning one's work and the work of those for whom one is responsible. At their simplest, performance appraisal systems enable the people who work in an organisation to plan and control their work better; to learn from their mistakes and profit from their successes; and to co-ordinate that work with the work of others with whom they interact.

It is quite easy to plod along comfortably in the average organisation, whether it be a profit-making industry, a service function, or a governmental or quasi-governmental institution. Handy, in an illuminating book[1], makes the point that in a bureaucracy it is more important that everyone perform to the same standard than that some people excel. Whether or not we work in a firm that could be described as a classical bureaucracy, we have all had experience of being told not to rock the boat. It is easier to make decisions that maximise one's comfort than decisions that maximise the firm's profits. It is easy to pursue courses that reflect well on one's own department, without thinking of the consequences for one's colleagues elsewhere: the salesman who lands production with an impossible set of targets, the design team who minimise capital outlay at the expense of later maintenance, the purchasing department who buy ill-fitting goods because they have not kept up-to-date on their real requirements. Yet, organisations need to learn; they need to keep abreast of the times, to inform themselves of the needs of tomorrow and the next decade. And to do this the managers in them need, from time to time, to consider their functions in a broad sense, away from the day-to-day pressures which will otherwise keep them focused on the short term. It is easy to confuse *urgency* with *priority*. Performance appraisal systems help get things the right way round.

Most people have an idea of what a performance appraisal system looks like. Once a year, or thereabouts, the manager meets with the subordinate in a quiet, undisturbed office.

Together they review the subordinate's performance over the last year. They may have a sheet of written objectives, or a job description, to help them to do this. The subordinate will not stay silent during this meeting; he will contribute quite a lot, perhaps the majority, of what is said. The review of performance may end with the manager assigning an overall performance rating to the subordinate, though whether he tells the subordinate what it is depends on the firm. The manager may also tell the subordinate about a salary increase, if this is appropriate.

The pair then spend a little time talking about the employee's present performance, and the jobs he is currently undertaking. They move from this to planning for the future; specific problem areas are identified, and plans made to overcome them. An effort is made to think of new opportunities which the employee could grasp. As they discuss these areas of performance, they evolve between them a view of how the employee's performance will be measured, and they also identify the difficulties which stand in his way, making plans wherever possible to overcome them. The plans may involve liaison with other departments, clarifying lines of responsibility; they may involve getting new information, or analysing old information a new way. Responsibility for acting on the plans is clearly identified during the interview.

From the specific requirements of next year's job targets they then move to more general conversation. Is there any training which either party can see the employee needing? Is there any special experience – a visit to another part of the firm, a project to work on – which would help him do his job better? Are there any skills he has which his job is not presently using? Can he think of ways in which the firm's performance as a whole could be improved? Where does he see his career going in this firm? What sort of job would he be best suited for after this one, and what training or experience does he require? All these questions lead to notes for action which are written into the record of the appraisal meeting, along with the manager's own view of the unused potential inside the employee.

No promises are made that promotion will result from the interview. The observant employee will have noticed that most of the discussion centred on his performance in his present job; most likely he will have noticed that performance appraisal interviews are routine in his firm, part of the day-to-day job of a manager and not a special procedure brought out when someone was to be assessed for promotability. If the interview was skilfully conducted, he will feel at the end of it that he has a greater insight into the job he has to do; a better idea of where it fits in the rest of the company; an increased awareness of the factors on which his performance is assessed, and an increased ability to monitor his own performance. He has had an opportunity to raise little points which niggle at him, and to ask questions in a free atmosphere. He knows what he can expect by way of training and development in the next year, and he knows that his manager is charged with the responsibility for putting this into practice.

And his manager, at the end of the interview, has a better understanding of the resources available to him. He has thought about the way in which he measures the performance of his people, and that has made him think again about his own job as manager. He has probably learned something about the appraisee which he did not know before. He has a better idea of the job the appraisee is doing; he has delegated responsibility, clearly, to the appraisee; he has tested potential trouble-spots in the appraisee or in the job. He, too, has learned something.

Now, performance appraisal systems have a multitude of purposes. As this book progresses the reader will see how many different functions in an organisation have fingers in the performance appraisal pie, and how many different purposes can be served during the interview and by the completion of the form. Above all purposes, though, one is paramount; the performance appraisal system is a tool for line managers, to enable them to do their job better. It is a means whereby they, and the people working for them, can learn from experience. If this purpose is not served, whole-heartedly, by the appraisal system, then all the others are built on an infirm foundation.

There was once an organisation where, in the course of routine monitoring of the appraisal system, it came to light that one manager had not done appraisals on certain of his subordinates for nearly ten years. When confronted with the evidence, he replied: 'Why should I do appraisals? The job has been the same for ten years, the man has stayed the same ... why should I bother going through a paper exercise?' In today's world, very few jobs stay the same, and people themselves change and develop. For the manager to think as he did, he had to construct for himself a very personal model of his managerial world – a model that was impervious to small changes, a model that did not allow him to learn, a model where information was processed to fit his preconceptions. When he learned, it would only be by crisis and catastrophe, never by gradual changes. No wonder he felt frightened of a performance appraisal system! Managers who are frightened of learning should not use an appraisal system; they might discover something new about themselves or their operation. They might have to change their opinions in the light of information given them by their subordinates. They might have to think about their jobs sufficiently hard that they delegate some of it. Perhaps – how awful! – they will discover that one of their subordinates has learned enough to be promoted. Managers who don't like learning will not like appraisal systems. One hopes that they are few. The rest of us regard appraisal systems as a means whereby the challenges of management can be met in a planned and controlled fashion.

The appraisal interview we described earlier will be familiar to readers who have had experience of appraisal systems; but in all probability the reader who is familiar with appraisal systems will recognise in that description aspects with which he is unfamiliar. Indeed, such is the wide variety of appraisal systems used that we devote much of this book to the problems of designing a system to suit one's unique requirements. When visiting firms we are often told 'Oh, it's just an ordinary performance appraisal system', only to discover that there are certain features we have not met before. Yet despite this wide variety of systems, there is little in the literature on appraisal which describes how a system is designed. Most of the guide-books start with the assumption that you have a system in and working. In consequence of this lack, there are many firms with an appraisal system that is not quite right; perhaps they bought a package deal from a consultant (some of them come with standardised paperwork, irrespective of whether you make motor cars or grow roses), or perhaps they hired a personnel specialist who transferred the system from his previous firm. Most appraisal systems, and most appraisal forms, have a high face validity – to the onlooker they appear to do the job suggested. Only when the system is in and working do some of the faults become obvious. If the reader has experienced an appraisal system that fell into disrepute, then perhaps it was because it had not been properly and economically designed in the first place. So, let us examine some of the purposes for which organisations use appraisal systems.

Purposes of appraisal systems

1 Feedback to appraisee

People do not improve on their results without feedback on their performance. Jobs vary in the extent to which they enable people to get accurate feedback. There are some jobs – mostly in service functions – where mistakes are easier to identify than successes. There are jobs involving customers or clients where people outside the organisation are a readier source of feedback than people inside. There are jobs of co-ordination, liaison, persuasion, working through other people, where the contribution of any one individual is difficult for him and others to identify. And people themselves vary in their ability to monitor their own performance and generate feedback for themselves; personality factors play a large part here, but it is difficult for anyone to monitor his own performance in a new job or a new firm. For some people, being deprived of feedback is a very stressful thing. Others may not give overt signs of minding very much, but they are still unlikely to learn. Performance appraisal systems help in at least two ways: first, by giving direct feedback from the manager to the employee (and vice versa), and secondly by helping the employee to set up ways of monitoring his own performance.

2 Management by Objectives

This is a system whereby the chief executive decides upon the objectives which the firm will try to attain, in the long term and then in the next year or so. Having set his targets, he considers the constraints acting to inhibit achievement of these targets, and also asks himself how he will be able to tell when they are being met. Then he meets the managers who report to him, either in a group or singly, and tells them his thoughts. Targets, constraints, and measures are discussed for each subordinate, and objectives are formally agreed. The subordinate managers then go away to repeat the process with their own subordinates, and so on down the line. In addition to the first meeting to agree objectives, a regular series of review meetings is held at each level, for checking progress and making alterations where appropriate.

When MbO works well, all the people in the organisation share a common goal, and common commitment. Delegation is encouraged. Rivalries and duplication of effort are reduced.

During disputes or times of uncertainty the laid-down statement of objectives serves as a useful reference point.

The appraisal system looks so much like MbO, especially to someone used to MbO, that it is important to specify resemblances and dissimilarities. The basic meeting – reviewing past progress and setting future targets – is common to both systems. MbO, however, assumes that the meetings are dependent on one another in a continuous chain, starting at the top. MbO assumes a formal sharing of objectives between manager and subordinate. In addition, some MbO systems generate a great deal of paperwork. Performance appraisal interviews can happen at any time, without waiting for the man at the top to begin the process. Objectives can be individual and personal, without any reference to the objectives of the appraising manager. And in practice there is a much wider variety of individual styles tolerated in performance appraisal systems than there is in MbO.

Much has been written on MbO, in praise and in criticism. It works well in sales and production departments, without much thought being given to it. It can be made to work in non-profit-making functions, in service areas, in matrix organisation; but to do this takes effort, and in the past this effort has not always been forthcoming. We therefore treat performance appraisal systems as separate from MbO, though the reader with experience of both will see the obvious parallels.

3   Salary review

At appraisal time the manager usually assigns an overall rating to the employee. Central salary planning functions find this rating useful to know, though there are organisations where salary grading is said to be a separate exercise. In fact, the link between performance appraisal and salary grading is controversial. Some experts believe that no mention of salary should be made during the interview; others say that salary should be discussed at the same time as the performance rating. And, irrespective of whether salary is discussed, there are those who say that a salary increase should follow soon after the interview, and others who say that it should be maximally distant.

Anyone studying the relationship between money and performance is soon struck by the large number of functions which money can fulfil – esteem, incentive, motivation, reward, freedom, status, etc. Part of the reason for the controversy surrounding any link between the appraisal interview and subsequent salary increase is the confusion about the different roles money can play. Centrally or locally, salary grading and performance appraisal have impact on each other.

4   Career counselling

The opportunity to talk about work plans for the next year or so opens up the option of talking more generally about the appraisee's career, his skills, his ambitions, and so on. For certain types of employee the need for good career counselling is obvious – the young specialist, for example, or the manager caught in a promotion blockage. Most people profit from a discussion about their training needs, needs they might have for new experiences or new skills to enable them to do their present job better and perhaps train for the next one. In performance appraisal interviews there is a deliberate attempt to look beyond the short term pressures and to ask what needs to be done in the medium and long term to maximise the employee's contribution.

5   Succession planning

At both the local and the central level there is a need to have available a list of people ready to take over in the event of a job becoming vacant. The appraisal system encourages managers to think about the abilities of their employees and to match these abilities with the known requirements of the job or jobs. This information is then collated, and it is possible to refine the system further by making sure that no employee 'covers' more than a given number of jobs, and that each job is 'covered' to a given depth. Succession planning is not the same as career counselling, though the two are often confused; career counselling is employee-based, whereas succession planning is job-based. Career counselling cannot be done without talking to the employee; succession planning very often is done without talking to the employee.

6   Maintaining equity

Most people have had experience of the situation where one man's unfavourable opinion of a subordinate has unfairly

influenced the subordinate's progress. The element of measurement implicit in most appraisal systems sometimes makes
employees fearful that any such unfairness is about to become
institutionalised. For this and other reasons many appraisal
systems involve the appraising manager's manager
('grandfather', as he is sometimes called) in the conduct of the
appraisal. He may have to sign off the appraisal form before the
interview, or afterwards, or both. He may actually take part in
the interview himself. He may be the first line of defence in case
of a dispute about the performance rating. Because he oversees
the appraisals of a number of different managers, he is in a good
position to see if any manager is idiosyncratic in his judgements,
and to intervene if necessary. When grandfathers are well
involved in the appraisal of their grandchildren, the
grandchildren very often feel more confident that equity is
maintained than with no appraisal system at all.

7 Hand-over between managers

A manager taking over a new team, or accepting a transfer from
another part of the firm, is greatly helped by having records of his
team's objectives, their past performance, and any special
problems or ambitions they may have. Firms expanding fast, by
internal growth or by acquisition, find the transition much easier
if new managers do not have to play themselves in from complete
ignorance each time. Indeed, the appraisal system can be a very
positive weapon in the hands of the central management team if
they are faced with the task of bringing some common standards
and practice to a group of companies which have merged.

8 To avoid trouble

Legislation in the UK and overseas is making it more and more
difficult to dismiss someone without being able to show records
of their unsatisfactory performance over a period of time,
together with evidence that the person concerned was given
adequate warnings and chances to improve. It is also more likely
that firms will have to justify their reasons for making a
particular promotion decision, if someone passed over by that
decision believes that unfair discrimination on the grounds of
race or sex was being practised. Even without these legislative
difficulties, many firms in high technology industries or in labour-
intensive organisations find that their managers' mistakes which

matter are mistakes with people. The growth of sophisticated management service departments, central planning functions, and so on, has removed managers' opportunities for mistakes in other areas; only in the mishandling of people are they still vulnerable.

It is a pity to have to recommend a tool like performance appraisal, which stands on its own as good management practice, and commend its usefulness in getting one out of trouble. But there is no doubt that performance appraisal systems have been used, and increasingly are used, as a way of handling poor performers so as to have the paperwork available to show an industrial tribunal.

Many more purposes can be added to that short list of eight. We shall come to a detailed breakdown later. The reader will see that the appraisal system can operate for *remedial action*, for *maintenance*, and for *development*. It is easy to see also how the line manager and the central planning functions each have an interest in the appraisal; sometimes it is not easy to see how the interests of the person being appraised are represented, but they are there nonetheless. Some of the problems of introducing and maintaining an appraisal system can be traced to uncertainty over who, exactly, the system is there to serve.

People involved in the appraisal process

Just as there are variations in the reasons why appraisal systems exist, there are variations in who is involved in the appraisal process. Some of the factors are:

1 Who is appraised? Some firms appraise managers only. Others appraise only above a given salary grade, or job level. In other firms everyone is part of the appraisal process. Sometimes people are allowed to drop out of the appraisal system, in whole or in part, because they are due for retirement soon and it is thought unnecessary to involve them in career counselling.

2 Who appraises? Most often, the immediate manager appraises. Grandfather sometimes shares the load; occasionally grandfather does it all. Sometimes a specialist viewpoint is sought, for example when a technical specialist is being appraised by a line manager who is not himself technically qualified to the same level. Rarely, the appraisals are carried out not by line managers, but by members of the central personnel function.

3   Who sees the records? Sometimes the appraising manager only; sometimes he and his manager; sometimes the personnel department also. Firms vary in the readiness with which they allow people to see their own appraisal records. There is also considerable variation in the way appraisal records are released to other managers; in some firms practically anybody senior to the appraisee can look at his records – if, for instance, they are searching for someone to fill a job; in others appraisal records are released on a strict 'need to know' basis, perhaps only with the employee's consent. It is likely that legislation and social pressures will soon influence the way appraisal records are handled.

Frequency and character

How often? Usually appraisals take place annually, as a matter of routine. In some firms the rhythm of the business dictates a more frequent appraisal pattern; it is rare to find intervals of longer than a year in which the appraisal process is taken at all seriously. Some firms allow an employee to refuse an appraisal, or to request one out of time, and instruct the manager to go along with the employee's wishes.

Who talks most? At one extreme, the employee comes to the interview well prepared and having structured his thoughts with the aid of a Preparation for Appraisal (or Preparation for Counselling) form. (A detailed description of such a form appears in Chapter Four.) During the interview he does most of the talking himself, with his manager taking a counselling role – though this does not mean that the employee automatically gets his own way. At the other extreme, no interview takes place at all unless the appraisee's performance is viewed by his manager as unsatisfactory.

Performance appraisal at work

There is no such thing as the universal performance appraisal system. What works well in one firm may work badly in another.

The system that works in the sales division may be totally inappropriate in service engineering. A system designed to give managers freedom of manoeuvre in motivating and controlling their employees may suddenly become inappropriate if the central planning department imposes new requirements on it, or if a pay freeze limits managers' discretion in giving salary increases. There is probably a place for every one of the variations we have listed above, and some more. We should however name the two prejudices we bring to the design of appraisal systems, thus:

Appraisal should not be operated selectively. We have little sympathy with the system in which only poor performers are invited in for interview. We also have little time for the practice (not often explicitly systematised) of appraising only high flyers. The opportunity to review one's performance coolly, in the light of experience, and without urgent time pressures, is so obviously beneficial for the individual concerned that we wonder about the survival characteristics of organisations where people are denied that opportunity.

Records should be open to the individual. This is a more controversial belief. Partly it is held because we believe that feedback on performance is desirable, and that seeing one's records is a way of getting such feedback. And partly it is held because of the reactions of managers who oppose openness. In discussion on appraisal systems we have often been confronted by a manager who flatly refuses to allow appraisees access to their records. When he is asked why, his objections boil down to a reluctance to justify the ratings given. Such an attitude indicates too great an emphasis on the remedial aspects of appraisal at the expense of the maintenance and developmental aspects, and also raises the question: why is he prepared to put marks on paper which he cannot defend? We shall return to the problem of open records systems later in this book.

The reader may also have his prejudices about appraisal systems, and if he himself is prejudice-free he may have to convince others of the utility of appraisals. Some of these prejudices may reflect unpleasant experiences with poorly designed appraisal systems in the past. The history of appraisal systems in the UK is worth study, as an indicator of the source of some common preconceptions.

Performance appraisal does have a history

It is difficult to state when the first appraisal system came into being in the UK. One of us, describing appraisal systems during an in-company seminar, was badly wrong-footed by a questioner who stated that appraisals were part of the law of master and servant! However, there was a clear surge of interest in the mid-sixties, often coinciding with the introduction of Management by Objectives systems. The Industry Training Boards encouraged many firms to develop appraisal systems, and often gave help in design and training. Inevitably when things went wrong with MbO, or when an ITB was not seen to be responsive to the commercial needs of the firm, the appraisal system suffered also; there are firms who tried appraisal systems ten years ago and have thrown them out, just as there are firms whose appraisal systems have worked smoothly for ten, fifteen, or even twenty years.

The introduction of legislation into the field of employment caused more attention to be paid to appraisal systems. The 1971 Industrial Relations Act cast a piercing glance at the procedures for dismissing poor performers, and some appraisal systems were designed specifically with the Act in mind; others were altered so that they could be registered as special procedures. It was not uncommon to find personnel departments very worried that the only people who were receiving appraisal interviews on time were the poor performers, which if perpetuated would have caused legal problems. Some people who were involved in such firms may remember performance appraisal as a paper exercise, with all sorts of pressures exerted by personnel department to keep the numbers up irrespective of the quality of the interviews.

A third influence on the growth of appraisal systems in the UK has been the multi-national employer – often American, often paternalistic (in the best and the worst senses), often anti-union. For such firms the appraisal system is a way of treating the employee as an individual, with a close working relationship with his boss based, ideally, on mutual respect. Such firms usually prefer payment by results, and the appraisal system provides a convenient vehicle for doing this. The appraisal system also allows a close monitoring of employee grievances, so that senior management can plan to maintain the high level of employee satisfaction for which such firms are known. The influence of the multi-national on the growth of appraisal systems has been both good and bad. On the one hand, the open advocacy offered by successful firms like IBM, Philips, Xerox, 3M, etc., makes it clear that these firms see performance appraisal as a means to commercial success, and as a tool for managing and developing entrepreneurs, rather than for punishing failures. On the other hand, the sheer size of such firms has led many smaller firms to think that appraisal systems are not for them.

This does not follow. Small and medium sized firms can develop their own appraisal systems, and in small firms the problems of big, old, computerised systems are avoided. The personnel officer in the small or medium firm may think that appraisal systems can only work in organisations the size of Shell or the Civil Service. Perhaps the most telling argument against this idea is the fact that in many large organisations the performance appraisal system is managed on a local basis. Mike Colbert, of British Airways, has described their appraisal and counselling system for some professional staff as a series of completely home-grown systems; the professionals in one group effectively designing and running their own system, with little reference to the systems operating in the rest of the organisation, and with a person from the central personnel function there to act as a resource in case things go wildly awry. Thus he has many small systems to look after; but, because they are small and locally developed they have the commitment of the people who designed them. In these circumstances, says Colbert, it is part of his job to live with the slight degrees of ambiguity created for him in the centre; a small price to pay for the high degree of commitment from the field force. Many large firms with a centrally designed system allow for local variations in the way the system operates, placing control in the hands of the local personnel expert. Thus an organisation-wide form may be used, but administration, running, advice, and perhaps training are all in the hands of the site personnel officer.

The problem is not one of getting appraisal systems into small firms when the small firms fear such systems can only be used by the big boys. The real problem is in getting the appraisal system in big firms to feel, to the managers who use it, like a small local system. You will not find in this book instructions on how to computerise your performance appraisal system; you will find advice on how to cut it down to a size where line managers feel it is a tool for them to use.

One objection commonly raised against appraisal systems is that they are merely institutionalising what a good manager does anyway. 'You're telling me to have a yearly review, going back twelve months, putting it all on paper, and having a special meeting to do it in? Nonsense, I see my chaps every day, I make a point of letting them know how they're going on, they all know where they stand without having a time-consuming interview.'

Sometimes this objection is carried further, for the sake of rhetoric. 'You seriously suggest I should save it all up and tell him once a year? If one of my chaps puts up a black he knows about it the minute it's happened, if I have anything to do with it.' Now of course we are not suggesting that performance appraisal is in any way a replacement for other good management practices, but it does have two unique contributions to make to the man–manager relationship:

Performance appraisal is a safety net. Surely, the good manager monitors, plans, and gives feedback as frequently as possible. The bad manager who has to be badgered by the performance appraisal into once a year giving thought to his people's performance and to plans for their future, will nonetheless do a better job than if he had been allowed to carry on without such prompting. And the busy manager, who would love to spend more time with his people and less time in fire-fighting, finds in the performance appraisal system open sanction for spending time with his appraisee. The system itself will not transform negligent managers into good ones, but its existence makes the managers' duties in this area more explicit. And an openly acknowledged system smooths the path for employees who do not think they are getting a fair deal in the matter of rewards, career development, personal recognition, etc.

Performance appraisal is a moment of privilege. A participant at a seminar, when the 'every good manager does it already' objection had been raised, responded by saying that the appraisal interview was a moment of privilege from which even the good manager and the satisfactory performer could benefit. Just as in a happy marriage there are some things which jar, though they are not worth mentioning in ordinary conversation, there are some things in the most satisfactory man–manager relationship which, if left alone, could go wrong and start to fester. At the appraisal interview there is a conscious, legitimate effort by both sides to clear the decks of all impediments; here the appraisee can say: 'You're a good boss in most ways, but I wish you wouldn't start a lot of non-urgent dictation at four-thirty on Friday,' and the boss can say: 'You're a good performer, but I wish you'd leave a note on your desk saying where you are when you're out of the office for any length of time.' Even when the main body of the appraisal interview is predictable, as far as both sides are concerned, there are still likely to be some surprises when the decks are cleared of every last impediment; and the value of this exercise cannot be over-stressed.

Summary

In this chapter we have considered the basic form of a performance appraisal interview, and looked at some of the variations in appraisal systems. We identified the various parties who have an interest in the appraisal system, i.e. the *appraiser*, the *appraisee*, and the *central planning* function. From a very brief history of appraisal systems in the UK we isolated some of the objections and unhappy memories that people may have, and tried to meet them, with particular emphasis on the need for the appraisal system to be small, and a tool for line managers to use.

2 Appraisal systems in action

All appraisal systems are unique. Any organisation that really *uses* its appraisal system – makes it contribute something towards the efficient running of the company – will have developed a system that suits the company culture. And as company cultures vary, so it is not possible to prescribe a universal system. In the previous chapter we outlined some of the many ways in which appraisal systems vary, and we stated that some people may have prejudices against appraisal systems because of unhappy experiences with ill-fitting appraisal systems. From this the reader will deduce that the differences in form of appraisal systems are related somehow to the differences in purposes, and he will expect a guide to these relationships. There is such a guide, in Chapter Four of this book, but we think it worthwhile to show the reader at this point some examples of appraisal systems in action so that he can evolve his own guide to the design of appraisal systems – if we show him the anatomy, he can deduce something of the physiology. In this chapter therefore we describe a selection of appraisal systems, taken from real life, neither outstandingly good nor outstandingly bad. As he reads the description of each system, the reader should ask himself questions such as: is this system remedial? What about maintenance and development? Who owns it? Who gets the most benefit out of it? Who gets the most information out of it? If it goes wrong, what will the symptoms be, and who is best placed to detect them? Thus, we trust, he will develop a feeling for the kinds of logic that later he will meet when we consider system design in general.

The A–Z Retailing Company Ltd

Every manager in this company is responsible for the conduct of performance appraisal interviews with his staff. Each employee is appraised once a year, on the anniversary of his joining the firm. Either party can request an appraisal at more frequent intervals; the employee can refuse such a request, the manager cannot. In practice the annual interval is fairly well adhered to. The manager is alerted to the need for the appraisal by the personnel department, where there is a system for automatically generating a list of appraisals due in the next month. A clean appraisal form is sent to the manager, with a copy of the previous year's form also. The manager has therefore up to a month to prepare himself for the interview. There is no automatic notification to employees that the appraisal is due, though most of them remember the month. The manager is supposed to make a formal appointment in plenty of time, but it often happens that employees are summoned into the manager's office for appraisal with little notice.

The interview is based on the appraisal form shown in Figure 2.1. This allows him to record simple information about the employee's performance during the past twelve months, with some further information about the employee's likely progress. The manager fills in all this information before the interview. As a matter of routine he passes the completed form to his manager before the interview takes place, and his manager is formally required to discuss with him any potential problems he sees – a poor performer, for instance, or someone in the wrong job. Mostly grandfather signs the form without comment.

Managers are advised to allow an hour for the interview, and most are completed well within the time. The interview takes place in his office, with the usual courtesies – telephone calls intercepted, no interruptions, as informal an atmosphere as possible. The manager begins by asking for the employee's view of his past year's work, and goes on to give his own views as he has structured them on the appraisal form, which, however, the employee is not allowed to see. They discuss in detail areas where their views differ, or where it is agreed that the employee's performance was poor. Having come to an agreement about the past, they go on to discuss the future; the manager suggests the objectives which the employee should try to achieve in the coming year. The appraising manager is supposed to refer to his own objectives when setting those for his employee, although there is not a formal Management by Objectives system. He is supposed to limit the objectives to not more than six in number, and not to try to cover the whole job by these objectives – he is picking out highlights, not writing a complete job description. The list of objectives, when complete, is copied out on blank paper and photocopied; one copy stays with the appraisee, one

THE A—Z RETAILING COMPANY LTD
APPRAISAL FORM

SURNAME:	INITIALS:	DATE:

JOB TITLE:	LOCATION:

Posts reporting directly to him:	Which post does the subject report to? How long has he been in his present job?

State briefly the specific objectives which were agreed for the 12 months under review; where none was set, list major tasks:	Summarise actual achievements and non-achievement of these. Be specific — quote examples. Indicate particular difficulties which he has faced.

	TRAINING NEEDS
What are his strengths as highlighted by his achievements during the period under review?	
What are the factors which could limit his development, as highlighted by his non-achievements during the period under review?	
Will he develop with the growth of his present job?	
What broadening assignments does he require?	

What are the training priorities you plan to implement for him?

Immediate Superior: Date:

Supplementary comment by Senior Manager:

Senior Manager: Date:

Fig. 2.1   Appraisal form used by the A—Z Retailing Company Ltd

with the manager, and one stays with the appraisal form when it is returned to the central personnel department.

Having settled next year's objectives, they spend a short time talking about the employee's progress in general next year – what sort of training does he want? what special experience? is there any help his manager should be giving him? They are not supposed to discuss the likelihood of specific promotions to the next job, but to concentrate on improving performance in the present job; inevitably, though, promotability and career prospects creep into the discussion. Neither are they supposed to talk about money, and this rule is fairly well adhered to. It is thought by the personnel depertment that discussion of money would colour the rest of the discussion so strongly that its utility would be lost.

The employee does not see his appraisal form, unless the manager shows it on his own initiative. There is no way in which the employee's comments can be recorded, though there is a grievance system which can be used if the employee wishes to make a strong point of his disagreement with what he believes to be written on the form. The appraising manager is supposed to tell his manager if the appraisal interview was not straightforward, and grandfather has the option to intervene himself if he thinks fit.

The completed forms are returned to the personnel department, who extract some simple information about training needs and return the document to store.

Comment

It is possible to deduce a number of things from this brief description of the A–Z's appraisal system. It is a modest system – it does not ask managers for complex or sophisticated judgements about personality, abilities, and potential. It looks back at last year's objectives, and forward to the next; there is no attempt made to compare one performer with another, or to apply company-wide performance criteria. It cannot conform to the classic MbO pattern, if for no other reason than that employees are appraised on the anniversary of their joining the company – the 'chain reaction' necessary for MbO cannot take place.

The A–Z system is not participative. Managers have a lot of

warning that the appraisal is due, and a chance to prepare themselves in writing; the appraisee knows roughly that the appraisal is due, but that is all. At the interview itself, it is likely – just from the very shape of the system – that the manager will do most of the talking. He is the better prepared, and he knows what he wants. Some of the motivational possibilities inherent in the appraisal system are lost by this means; in fact, the manager is set up to talk, not to listen. If he wants to alter the appraisal in any way after the interview, he has to make a special effort; there is no automatic provision for him to wait until he hears what the employee has to say.

The employee is likely to feel a little lost in the system. The appraisal happens *to* him, not *with* him. He knows that a report on his performance is being submitted by his manager, but he does not know what is written on it and he does not feel that he has any discretion in the matter of what goes on the report. If he is working in an area where success is reasonably easy to identify, sales or production, for instance, he may feel that the objective-setting part of the exercise is a foregone conclusion. If he works in an area where it is more difficult to describe success and failure, a service function, or middle management, for instance, he may feel the objectives bear little relationship to what he has actually to achieve.

The reader can probably think of a number of improvements he would like to make to the A–Z appraisal system so that some of the parties concerned could get more positive benefit from it.

Cloud, Cuckoo & Partners Ltd

This large organisation, with a wide range of commercial interests, has an appraisal system that fully reflects the complexity of its business. As in the previous example, appraisals are conducted annually by the employee's manager, but only managers and certain kinds of high grade specialist are appraised. The appraisal is not made with objectives in mind, however; instead the manager has to fill in a series of scales describing the attributes of the person being appraised. This set of scales is given in Figure 2.2. In addition the appraising manager fills in details of the employee's present and previous positions and technical qualifications, and gives details of the

Section II

KNOWLEDGE OF WORK RELEVANT TO PRESENT POSITION

Does he have a clear understanding of his job and a working knowledge of Company practices and policies? Does he have the experience necessary to carry out his work effectively

COST CONSCIOUSNESS

Has he an appreciation of cost control? Does he understand the need for proper utilisation of labour, materials and plant?

ANALYTICAL ABILITY AND JUDGEMENT

Does he think problems through and come to sound, logical conclusions? Does he show creative imagination in proposing new methods?

RESOURCEFULNESS AND INITIATIVE

Can he overcome difficulties without detailed instruction? Does he have ideas of his own and are they realistic?

ABILITY TO DELEGATE

Does he successfully apportion responsibilities and corresponding authority?

DRIVE AND ENERGY

Is he diligent and persistent in carrying out work assigned? Does he apply himself with enthusiasm and with good purpose?

ACCEPTABILITY

Does he get on with other people? Does he command respect and co-operation?

ABILITY TO INSPIRE CONFIDENCE

Does he have natural leadership qualities? Does he have an assured manner which earns the confidence of others?

PERSONAL APPEARANCE

In relation to his job is he neat, clean and appropriately dressed?

MORAL COURAGE AND STABILITY

Does he accept responsibility and stand by his decisions?
Does he maintain self control in all situations?

ASSESSMENT OF PERFORMANCE

Does he achieve his targets?
Consider the main objectives of his job over the last 12 months

EFFECTIVENESS IN PRESENT POSITION   Outstanding   More than adequate

Fig. 2.2   Scales describing the attributes of the appraisee on the appraisal form used by Cloud, Cuckoo & Partners Ltd

☐	☐	☐	☐	☐
Outstanding	Above average	Adequate	Somewhat below standard	Deficient

☐	☐	☐	☐	☐
Outstanding	Very good	Adequate	Lacks proper sense of values	Wasteful

☐	☐	☐	☐	☐
Excellent	Very good	Satisfactory	Somewhat below average	Unsatisfactory

☐	☐	☐	☐	☐
Outstanding	Frequently takes initiative	Satisfactory in most situations	Sometimes lacking in initiative	Needs detailed instructions

☐	☐	☐	☐	☐
Excellent	Very good	Adequate	Rarely delegates	Tries to do everything himself

☐	☐	☐	☐	☐
Unusually industrious and energetic	Sustained application	Works well. Usually with good purpose	Sometimes fails to apply himself	Lazy—needs constant supervision

☐	☐	☐	☐	☐
Excellent	Very good	Quite acceptable	Rather difficult	Awkward and unco-operative

☐	☐	☐	☐	☐
Inspires great confidence	A very good leader	Satisfactory	Not too sure of himself	Weak, easily led

☐	☐	☐	☐	☐
Excellent impression	Very favourable impression	Suitable	Not sufficiently careful	Untidy

☐	☐	☐	☐	☐
Outstanding	Above average	Average	Rather unstable	Weak

Outstanding. Always recognises his targets and achieves them ☐	Endeavours to deal with everything that comes along—sometimes fails to meet objectives ☐	Satisfactory but tends to concentrate on high priorities only ☐	Does not always understand his objectives and fails to meet targets ☐	Spends too much time on inessentials, fails to identify and meet main objectives ☐

☐	☐	☐	☐
Adequate	Barely adequate	Inadequate	Unproved

employee's suitability for promotion on a four-point scale, thus:

Ready for immediate promotion to...
Not quite ready for promotion because...
Far from ready for promotion because...
Unlikely to be suitable for promotion because...

The manager also makes recommendations for training or other broadening experience.

The appraisal interview is initiated in a similar fashion to the previous example – by a reminder to the manager from the personnel department in time for him to prepare himself. It is obvious, however, from the set of scales shown that the appraisal interview is more likely to concentrate on the employee's personal characteristics than on his job objectives. There is no formal setting of next year's objectives, nor any reviewing of last year. The employee does not see the form at any time, so the impetus for beginning the interview is with the manager. However, in practice most managers find it difficult to base an interview on the performance rating implied by these scales, and in consequence most of the interviews are short and not particularly searching. There is some forward planning in the discussion of training and other experience, but most of this part of the form concentrates the manager's mind on the employee's suitability for promotion to the next job rather than on improvement in the present job. Some of the managers worry about the implication that people rated as unsuitable for immediate promotions are somehow deficient.

Completed forms go to the personnel department, where they are used in succession planning. A list of people thought suitable for promotion to particular jobs is assembled, so that when a vacancy occurs the listing can be sent to the appointing manager, who then asks to see the appraisal records of likely candidates. There is, however, no compulsion to appoint from this list. In addition to succession planning, the list is used for extraction of training needs by the training department.

Comment

The system adopted by Cloud, Cuckoo & Partners shows some of the more common mistakes made when designing an appraisal system. The long list of scales describing personality characteristics is, in practice, almost impossible to operate. It is usually difficult to get two people to agree on what is meant by some of these scales – acceptability, or personal appearance, for example – and this lack of agreement would cause difficulty when one manager had to use another manager's rating if all ratings were taken at their face value. In fact most appraising managers played safe when making their ratings and it is unusual to find people given a poor rating. In the actual appraisal interview most managers feel too embarrassed to begin with a discussion of another adult's personal qualities, whether they have rated them high or low, and so most interviews are sketchy affairs in which one or two outstanding issues are discussed but an overall coverage of the previous year is not attempted. We have already seen that the appraisal form does not guide the parties towards a systematic discussion of the following year.

The set of scales which constitutes the bulk of the appraisal form also has one glaring fault in its layout – the points on the scale are so placed that a poor performance rating can be given without moving one's hand across the page. This is an encouragement to hasty ticking of scales as one moves to the bottom of the paper.

Cloud, Cuckoo's system worked well for them for a while. During a period when the business was expanding almost of its own accord; when there were no major technological changes and no major changes in market conditions; and when employees were content to work on the 'good chap' system of performance appraisal, Cloud, Cuckoo's system caused them no problems. No one worried about the looseness with which the scales were derived and defined, because there was a general consensus about the kind of up-and-coming man they should be looking for. However, a massive change in market conditions left them unable to use the performance appraisal system as before – the type of man they wanted had changed, and the appraisal system's lack of precision was apparent. Then the market stopped growing and they suddenly had to think about career development in a time when promotions were not easily forthcoming. The appraisal system's implicit judgement that people should be preparing for the next job again brought them trouble as it was realised that people would have to stay in their present jobs for much longer. The blow which will probably kill Cloud, Cuckoo's appraisal system in its present form is the legislation on employment protection and unfair dismissal; someone rated poorly may be able to claim that the poor rating was due, not to his performance, but to the fact that 'his face didn't fit'.

Money Brothers

Money Brothers is a City firm, a partnership which began as a firm of accountants and spread into other areas including business consultancy. At the moment the accountancy and the consultancy side work closely together, though they are under nominally different management. Young, bright people join them as accountants or as (usually) management service specialists; move around from assignment to assignment within the firm; and a large number of them leave in their late thirties to take up positions in line management in other companies. The peculiar laws governing partnerships in the UK affect the way Money Brothers is managed. In addition, the nature of the work is such that a system of matrix management is judged to be the best for operational efficiency. Matrix management is a system whereby teams are organised according to the project they are undertaking at the time, with little or no regard for factors such as seniority or grading. Reporting relationships may shift from one project to another, so that the manager of one project may find himself in a subordinate role on another project even though the personnel remain the same. (There is an excellent summary of matrix management techniques in Knight[1].) In Money Brothers an almost pure matrix system operates, with a small tendency to let seniority override ability when deciding who is to manage certain projects. Even the most senior partners have operational tasks, and their own clients, to distract from the monotony of management meetings.

It is obvious that neither the A–Z system nor the Cloud, Cuckoo system would work for Money Brothers. Both these systems depend upon there being a fixed hierarchy through which appraisals are conducted. Both firms place full responsibility for the appraisal on the man's line manager. In addition it could reasonably be inferred from their appraisal forms that they expect people to remain with the firm and grow through the firm – leaving at age 35 would appear disloyal, perhaps.

In Money Brothers all performance appraisals are carried out by one man, a personnel professional who is also familiar with the technical aspects of both accountancy and management consulting. At the end of each project, the project manager writes a short summary of the performance of each of the people who have worked for him, listing the skills required, the degree of diligence needed, the difficulty of the project, and any demands on non-specialist skills such as political sensitivity. These assessments are not shown to the people concerned at the time. No one below a certain level of seniority can make assessments, but such people do not often find themselves managing projects. The assessments are collated centrally, and the development manager (as he is known) assembles a file on each man. As he does so he inevitably comes to know the particular habits of each rater – some are lenient, some scrupulous, some unobservant. Then, once a year, he interviews each of the people for whom he has responsibility. Before the interview he compiles a composite performance appraisal summary for the last year, and this is sent to the man before the interview. In addition the development manager may do some preparatory work by investigating further (with the project manager concerned) any outstanding features of the appraisee's performance.

The appraisal interview itself consists of feedback on performance, counselling, and developmental guidance. There is much more need for feedback on performance in a matrix management scheme, especially in consultancy where one is working for a client rather than a colleague. Because the development manager himself did not have charge of the individual projects which form the basis of the appraisal, it is not possible for the interview to deteriorate into a 'Yes I did' – 'No you didn't' argument, and any disagreements about performance are addressed by the development manager in counselling style, with the appraisee doing most of the talking. Nor can the development manager take a directive role in planning for the future, because he does not direct the work. Next year's work is difficult to plan in a consultancy. But they can, and do, talk about the range of experience the appraisee needs, the training and development he requires, the variety of projects on which he hopes to work. After the interview the development manager takes a firm hand in directing this experience; it is his job to ensure that people are broadened and given variety rather than consistently assigned to the type of project where they have shone before. And finally they spend some time talking about the appraisee's career – not just in Money Brothers, but his career in general. The firm has realised that it can do nothing to prevent the high labour turnover among people in their mid-thirties, and that this may be to their ultimate advantage – lose a bright EDP specialist to become data-processing manager of a medium sized firm, and he may bring you his management consultancy work afterwards. So, their career counselling really is *career* counselling, not just career in Money Brothers.

Comment

It is often said that performance appraisal systems do not work outside hierarchical systems. Yet in Money Brothers we have an example of a system that appears to work well. It provides one or two unique services which the staff of Money Brothers would not get any other way; detailed and considered feedback on performance, and an honest broker to negotiate training and job enrichment. Lack of these two things often causes great discontent amongst professionals in client-based services. The weakness of Money Brothers' system is partly its dependence upon the quality of the development manager, and partly the very rarity of a system like theirs. When the development manager is a strong personality, getting genuine satisfaction out of helping people to achieve more, and possessing all the skills of counselling and listening and the ability to read accurately between the lines of other people's judgements, then the system works well. He will be respected by the people he counsels, and will not have his judgements swayed by considerations of day-to-day office politics. If the position of development manager is given to someone without these qualities – if for example it were given to a regular Money Brothers consultant who eventually wished to return to active consultancy – then the system would deteriorate into a paper exercise. And it would be difficult to get good advice on improving the system, because most such advice would assume an ordinary hierarchical organisation.

Matrix management systems are not often found outside groups of specialists. Money Brothers contain excellent specialists and had the foresight to recruit one of high quality for their development manager. That their appraisal system works is a clear indication that it isn't the system that's the answer, it's the people who run it.

Red Tape

In contrast with Money Brothers we offer an example of an appraisal system gone wildly wrong through choking in its own bureaucracy. The problem began when the manager of a 54-year-old technician noticed that the man had become unnaturally quiet and depressed. The manager grew alarmed at what he thought were suicidal tendencies and tried to discover what was the matter. He was violently rebuffed. When the problem persisted he enlisted the help of his own manager and local personnel specialists, who finally got to the root of the problem.

Some months previously, the manager – then newly promoted and as yet untrained – had to fill in performance appraisal reports on his team. These reports were not to be shown to the people concerned. An overall performance rating was made, on a six-point scale. The sixth box indicated an unsatisfactory performance calling for formal remedial action, and managers were under instruction not to tick that box without discussion with the subordinate. The fifth box carried no such obligation; it was labelled to describe people whose performance was just adequate. The manager ticked this box in respect of the technician, because he thought this was an honest appraisal of the man.

It is not clear what happened next. The performance appraisal forms were sent to the central personnel unit, and someone in that unit initiated the unsatisfactory performance report (UPR) procedure. The manager and his manager believe that this was deliberately done by personnel people taking it upon themselves to correct managers' known leniency in giving ratings. In the personnel department this is denied and the action put down to a clerical error. In any event, the full weight of the UPR procedure descended on the technician, who had not had any warning of a meeting with his manager; the first he knew was a letter telling him, in effect, that he had two months to improve or be fired, or at least downgraded. It was this letter that caused his depression, and his belief that his manager had initiated it accounted for the hostile reception with which the manager's solicitous enquiries were treated. As part of the UPR procedure there was an interview with a personnel specialist, who was not familiar with the technician's work and who tried to engage him in an attempt to set standards of performance which bore little relevance to his daily tasks. Meanwhile his manager, and *his* manager, were trying to bring a stop to the UPR procedure before it did further damage; in this organisation the personnel department are responsible for appointment, transfer, and placement, and the manager feared that his technician would be fired or downgraded unless he acted. It proved almost impossible to get the personnel department to admit that there was something wrong with their system; no one person responsible for the appraisal system could be found with authority sufficient to wipe the slate clean. After weeks of persuasion the manager succeeded in bringing to an end the 'fire or downgrade' procedure, but that was all. *Two years* after the problem began, the technician and his manager were getting routine letters through the system asking if his performance had improved sufficiently to take him off probation; the letters may still be arriving as we write. The technician has not enough years to retirement for him to move to another job, or for his manager sensibly to suggest it. Instead he remains embittered, and his effect on the morale of the rest of the department can easily be imagined.

Comment

All the case studies in this chapter are true. This one illustrates what happens when the system uses the people, instead of the people using the system. It so happens that there are many aspects of Red Tape's appraisal system which we applaud; the actual performance criteria on appraisal forms are based on sound research, there is a comprehensive training system, much attention is paid to the involvement of managers up and down the line and to the appraisal of mediocre performers, etc. Yet the system, once installed and computerised and given into the charge of a department whose job was to follow instructions rather than *manage* the system, became a monster; and the designer of this very system has often gone into print about the design of appraisal systems!

Big appraisal systems are dangerous if they become centrally managed and if the central people see their priorities as not rocking the boat rather than responding to the needs of the periphery. *Old* appraisal systems are dangerous if the people who designed them, and the purposes for which they were designed, are outdated, gone, or forgotten. *Computerised* systems are dangerous if there is no one available to make a quick executive decision that will override computer error or human error.

Hardware International

In this firm everyone is part of the performance appraisal scheme, which centres on annual interviews between employee and manager. The computer in the personnel department alerts the manager to the need for an appraisal interview; it also alerts the subordinate, and sends him a form on which he can prepare himself for the appraisal interview. Thus both employee and manager have a chance to prepare themselves before they meet, though the employee is under no obligation to fill in his form and does not have to show it to his manager. The manager has prepared a draft of the part of the appraisal form which reviews past performance, but he has not written it into the appraisal form itself.

The interview begins by looking backward, the manager asking for the subordinate's evaluation of his own performance and his reasons. Because of the preparation for counselling form the employee is well equipped to start the conversation, and this makes the interview less like the formal reading of a charge sheet. The manager is expected to show the employee his final written summary of the review of last year's performance against objectives, though he does not start the interview with it. The manager must also record any areas of disagreement remaining about their evaluation of last year's work.

As well as reviewing performance against specific objectives, the manager has a short list of scales on which to record performance in general. Overall performance is rated from 1 to 5, thus:

1 Exceeds requirements in all respects
2 Exceeds requirements in most respects
3 Exceeds requirements in some respects
4 Meets basic requirements of job
5 Fails to meet basic requirements

and there are other scales on which the manager rates aspects of performance such as clarity of communication, speed of response, level of general knowledge, etc. The employee is able to see these ratings. There is also an opportunity for the manager to state whether the employee's performance has materially altered during the past six weeks.

The interview, and the form, move on to planning for future performance in the present job. Up to six objectives are to be set and agreed, together with standards of performance against which achievement is to be measured. Training or development to do the present job better is also discussed, and the conclusions recorded. The manager then draws the employee into a broader discussion of his hopes and ambitions. These, together with the manager's view of the employee's potential for promotion, are recorded on the only part of the form which the employee cannot see. It is thought that if he saw the judgement of his potential (which is made on a single scale of how long before he will be ready for promotion) then he would read into this the promise of a job. So the manager fills in the last part of the form after the actual interview; but at the end of the interview itself he gives the partly completed form to the employee for him to write any comments that he might have. The employee signs to say that he is satisfied (or both parties record their disagreement and take it to grandfather for further discussion).

After the interview a copy of the form goes to the central personnel department. Trends in matters such as training needs, sources of discontent, or employee ambitions are noted, but the responsibility for (say) nominating a man to a training course rests with the line manager. Information on promotability is put into the manpower planning system. Overall performance grades are extracted and used in salary planning, etc. But the forms themselves stay with the appraising managers. Each manager is encouraged to use the appraisal system for day-to-day management; by setting a series of short term objectives to help someone in need of coaching, for example, or to help in planning whom to assign to a particular team. In the event of someone performing below standard, the appraisal interview – with special emphasis on objective-setting – is repeated at frequent intervals. This serves two purposes; it is more likely that improvement will occur if it is seen to be managed, with short term goals and regular reviews; and if that improvement does not occur within a reasonable time, a written record is available in the event of an action for unfair dismissal.

Comment

Hardware International's is one of the better performance appraisal schemes. It reviews *performance*, not personality or likeability. The performance review centres on the setting of specific objectives, so that the appraisee can monitor his own performance by using the agreed measures. It makes clear distinctions between performance in the past, performance now, and future performance. The preparation for counselling form (about which more later) increases the chance that the employee will come to the interview prepared and ready to talk. And the subsequent use of the appraisal records is evenly divided between the central personnel function and individual line managers.

Their system is by no means perfect, of course. Strong objection can be raised against the practice of assessing potential by reference to present performance in present job. Some managers dislike the length of time the interviews take – two hours is not unusual, though Hardware argue that any interview with genuine dialogue is unlikely to take less, and that the employee merits two hours' undivided attention once a year. A further difficulty is that in common with many organisations which have had appraisal systems for some time, Hardware finds that its managers often have difficulty in counselling about personal development during a slow-down in economic growth. They do, however, regularly monitor employee attitudes to the appraisal system, and to other aspects of their employment policies; at present employee satisfaction with the system is pleasingly high, and if past record is reliable then should employees become dissatisfied with the system it would be changed.

Some principles

The five systems described represent only a small range of the options available when designing an appraisal system. Though the basic pattern remains the same, the variations are many. Figure 2.3 summarises some of the main variations in appraisal systems as they appear to an outsider studing the system for the first time. If the reader can obtain them, it is instructive to take a selection of appraisal forms and go through them, asking what they tell one about the appraisal system, just as we have done in our five examples. The reader with an existing system should take his appraisal form and ask: 'What would suffer if we dropped this question from the form?' or 'What would the consequences be if this question were not answered well?' One's own answers can sometimes be illuminating.

There are some general principles beginning to emerge. The presence of rating scales on an appraisal form implies a need to compare between employees. Perhaps this is for job evaluation, or for salary planning. Perhaps it is to enable better searches to be carried out when succession plans are made. Perhaps it is to help monitor the effects of training, or of another outside

All staff eligible   Managers and salaried staff only

Line manager appraises   Personnel specialist appraises
Technical specialist appraises   Grandfather appraises

Employee sees all the form   Employee sees some of the form
                          Employee sees none of the form

Self-appraisal or preparation for counselling form used
Self-appraisal or preparation for counselling form not used

Past performance only measured
Past performance and present performance measured

Measurement against performance targets or objectives
Measurement against rating scales of performance
Measurement against rating scales of personality
No measurement criteria specified

Presence or absence of rating scales, and number of divisions

Opportunity to set targets for future performance

Discussion of training and development needs for present job
Discussion of training and development needs for next job
Discussion of training and development needs long term

Manager rates potential on one-dimensional scale
Manager rates potential on multi-dimensional scale
Manager makes no formal rating of potential

Discussion of salary is forbidden
Discussion of salary is mandatory
Discussion of salary is optional

Frequency and regularity of appraisal interviews

Disputes resolved by appeal to grandfather
Disputes resolved by appeal to personnel
No procedure for resolving disputes

Who may see appraisal forms, and for what purpose?

Use of forms for central planning purposes

Use of forms for day-to-day management and coaching purposes

Fig. 2.3   The main variations in appraisal systems.

change. Some comparison is anyway implied. An alternative to rating scales is a series of key words, after which the appraising manager writes a sentence or two summarising the employee's performance in this area. Firms using this method are, one deduces, less interested in comparing between employees and more interested in constructing a detailed picture of the employee (and his manager). Both points of view are valid, though they represent different philosophies of appraisal. And, both types of appraisal form could be asking pertinent questions or asking questions totally unrelated to success in the job, depending upon where the rating-scales or prompt-words came from. Some firms base their rating scales on empirical research by the personnel department. Others have a committee meeting, with the inevitable result that the scales or prompt-words have an impreciseness that is the result of committee and compromise. Still other firms take trait names or rating scales from the appraisal forms of other organisations, with or without adaptation to their own needs.

Looking at a variety of appraisal systems, one can make deductions from the way they use the grandfather figure. When he is much involved, one infers a concern for equity between appraising managers. If he is the first line of defence in a dispute, rather than the dispute automatically coming to the personnel department, then one infers that the designers of the system wanted to keep the system in the hands of line managers as much as possible.

The degree of employee involvement, as shown by the presence of preparation for counselling forms, space for the employee to write his comments on the appraisal form, and whether the employee is allowed to see the form, tells the experienced observer a great deal about the *balance* in the appraisal system between motivation and control. At one extreme we have self-appraisal systems, where the information and discussion are brought to the interview by the employee; at the other extreme we have the read-aloud charge sheet, or the system where one only knows one's rating if it is unsatisfactory. The degree of employee involvement also tells one something about the maturity of the managers who use the appraisal system – whether they like learning, whether they can listen, whether they can give their employees the credit for a job well done.

One can look at the appraisal form to see how much data the

central planning people extract from it – salary planning, training planning, succession planning, relocation, wastage studies, information with which to validate their selection techniques, and so on. It is for these reasons that questions appear on appraisal forms asking the manager to record basic demographic information about the employee, or other questions not immediately related to the job in hand. One cannot infer much about the man–manager relationship from such questions, but studying them on a strange appraisal form is nonetheless valuable – it forces the question: 'Who uses this information, and what for?' Appraisal forms, like attitude surveys and job application forms, sometimes get littered with official-looking questions for which there is no real purpose. When there are a great many such questions on the form, it begins to look like a child of the personnel department, and not a tool for line management at all. And if, after looking at his appraisal system and discarding questions that have no explicit purpose, the reader finishes up with a one-page form and four questions only, then so be it. Tools can only be designed when one knows what they will be used for.

Summary

It is possible to make inferences about the way an appraisal system works, and what it feels like to those taking part, by examining the associated paperwork. Five systems have been so examined, in varying degrees of detail, and the consequences pointed out. Major variations include the degree of participativeness in the interview; the choice of comparison group, and the way the employee is compared if a comparison is required; and the use of data by central planning functions.

3 Installing a system: performance criteria

Having looked at some appraisal systems to give the reader an impression of the problems of design and maintenance implicit therein, we now come to the basic questions of planning an appraisal system: given a blank sheet of paper, where does one start?

As all appraisal systems involve performance criteria, we shall start here, progressing in later chapters to the problems of system design, maintenance, and training. Even systems where managers are left to supply the performance criteria for themselves – and such systems do exist – rely to a certain extent on guidance and monitoring from the personnel function.

Looking back over the appraisal systems described in the previous chapter, the reader will see that performance criteria fall into basically three different kinds: *personality* characteristics, *performance* characteristics, and attainment of *objectives*. The first two kinds are usually applied across a variety of appraisees, perhaps the whole organisation; objectives can be set for an individual with no reference to any other appraisee. Examples of personality measures include *drive, loyalty, integrity, acceptability*, etc., examples of performance measures include *accuracy, clarity, analytical ability, delegation*, and so on. In recent years there has been a strong trend away from the former kind of measure towards more performance-based measures: a change that is discussed in full in Williams[1], Campbell et al.[2], and Gill et al.[3]. In some cases organisations have switched from the one measure to the other because of overt employee pressure to be measured by results rather than on personality.

Opinions among experts strongly favour the performance-based type of measure, for a number of reasons. One very good reason is that it is notoriously difficult to get appraising managers to agree on what is meant by a personality-type word; they are therefore not measuring to common standards, as employees soon discover if they have a change of manager. Another objection is the extent to which a number of personality measures depend on the interaction between appraiser and appraisee; the appraiser's own personality entering into the judgement more than is acceptable. Yet another objection is often voiced by employees as: 'What does it matter what sort of chap I am as long as I do the job right?' This is a difficult objection to deal with, especially as there are borderline cases where personality does play some part – the appearance of salesman, and the cheerfulness of a nurse, have both been raised in industrial tribunals lately. It seems that where personality factors do play some part in a person's effectiveness, they should at least be clearly defined, to the point where the appraising manager's judgement can be clearly replicated by anyone else.

Another possible objection to personality measures is implicit in Hunt's study of management attitudes and practices towards women at work[4]. In a very thorough study, she asked personnel and other managers to rate the likelihood that men and women would show each of a given list of characteristics. The list was chosen to be as thorough and wide ranging as possible. Hunt's thought provoking discovery was that, *whatever* the characteristic, women were judged less likely to show it than men. From this illustration of the roots of prejudice it is easy to draw the conclusion that if judgements are to be made about people at work then the appraising managers must be given all possible assistance to make those judgements fairly and objectively.

Looking over the literature, and the borderline cases that have come to industrial tribunals, we conclude that the criteria on which performance is appraised *must* satisfy the following guidelines:

(a) they must be genuinely related to success or failure in the job;
(b) they must be amenable to objective, not subjective, judgement.

In addition it is helpful if some or all of the following guidelines are also satisfied:

(a) they must be easy for the manager to administer;
(b) they must appear fair and relevant to the employee;
(c) they must strike a fair balance between sensitivity to the needs of the present job, and applicability to the company as a whole.

If these conditions are met, the chance of running into serious trouble with one's performance criteria will be reduced. Managers will find the appraisals easier to make, and employees are more likely to feel that the system is fair and helpful. Handover between managers and transfer of employees will be easier, and the central control function will be storing data of known usefulness and consistency.

Deriving performance measures

The first of our guidelines was that performance criteria must be genuinely related to success or failure in the job. Getting a list of such performance criteria is not an easy task, and the bulk of this chapter is given over to ways in which the reader can discover by empirical research the relevant criteria for his organisation. First, though, a cautionary tale about how not to derive performance criteria.

The organisation concerned is staffed mainly by highly expert specialists who have no appraisal system of their own. Their assistants, who are not so highly qualified, have been agitating for an appraisal system for some time. A committee was set up to deliberate on the appropriate performance criteria. No empirical research was done, and by the usual processes of committees a list of characteristics was arrived at. That list itself reflected the power struggles and compromises that had gone on in the committee; however, when the list was published the experts – whose *assistants* the list referred to – objected. The list contained criteria of performance which, said the experts, implied that their assistants could from time to time make an expert contribution; the experts were not prepared to see that happen. As a result of their pressure the list was amended yet again, thus losing one of its most relevant performance criteria. As the committee concerned has put in an inordinate number of hours designing the system, the system is unlikely to be abandoned; but its utility is doubtful.

We give this illustration for a number of reasons. First, to warn against using a committee of personnel experts to design the criteria; there is no guarantee that the list will emerge in a form that line managers can use. Secondly, to caution against compromise; merging characteristic A with characteristic B to satisfy the needs of two pressure groups may indeed satisfy them, but the resulting characteristic C is unlikely to be defined clearly and usefully.

Groups of people can make a useful contribution to the derivation of performance criteria, if they are the people doing the
actual job being appraised. In one firm, for example, the personnel manager visited various locations to hold informal discussions with staff, asking them the question: 'How would you like
your performance to be measured?' No promises were given on
the spot, of course, but they were able to put together a useful-
looking list which had the merit of being acceptable to most
employees. They say that the finished list contained one or two
measures which they in the personnel department would not
have thought of, and that, as often happens, employees set higher
standards for themselves than management would have offered.

Part of the value of this exercise was its contribution to public
relations. We suggest that the reader who contemplates designing an appraisal system from scratch, or a thorough re-design of
the existing system, should also conduct some empirical research
into performance criteria, using one or more of the methods outlined below.

Critical incident

Interview a random sample of employees in the area to be
covered by the performance appraisal, asking them to tell you
about the most difficult problem or incident they have had to
deal with over a specified period of time. (The time period varies
with the complexity of the job; one week for routine jobs, six
months for research laboratories.) Take down all the details – who, when, where, what with, how frequently, at what
cost? For the sake of symmetry you may also ask about an incident that has gone well, but this question is unlikely to yield so
much data. Then analyse the incidents to look for trends, common factors, etc. The results of this analysis translate very easily
into performance measures for the appraisal system.

An example will illustrate. In a service engineering section of a
firm manufacturing and selling capital equipment, there was dissatisfaction with the performance measures. The existing measures concentrated on machine performance, technical ability,
and the amount of time spent machine-fixing. The engineers
thought that this did not fully reflect the demands of their jobs.
After critical incident interviews it became apparent that many
of the critical incidents did not involve technical skills at all, but
skills of (i) liaison with people in other functions, and (ii) cus-

tomer relations. In particular it was shown that where lost business had resulted from the critical incidents it was the engineer's lack of interpersonal rather than technical skill which was at fault. As a result the performance appraisal system was modified to include these non-technical skills, and considerable improvements were noted.

Critical incident technique is unlikely to give all the information required in setting performance standards. It is, in Pareto terms, a way of getting at the 20 per cent of the incidents that cause 80 per cent of the problems. It helps to set priorities. It helps to identify areas that should be measured but which are in an organisational blind spot. And it helps to analyse performance characteristics in areas where they are indistinct, such as service functions, middle management. Also, because one can ask what each incident *cost* (lost business, lost people, lost reputation, lost morale, etc.) one can back up one's argument with figures. It is easy to do, with the additional advantage of being empirical research in the field rather than armchair research in the personnel department.

Content analysis of working documents

This is a method of setting performance standards by going over relevant existing documents to discover the standards people are actually using; the things they consider important; and the standards people are failing to meet. The field of content analysis is so wide that we can only indicate some possible applications here; a fuller review is found in Stewart[5], and we strongly recommend Webb et al. *Unobtrusive Measures*[6] as a readable and informative guide to the use of background information for research.

The principle is simple. Having gained access to the necessary documents (e.g. working files, performance records, customer complaint letters, minutes of meetings) go through them systematically. You can ask a number of questions, e.g. What skills are being demonstrated by these people? or What skills are lacking in these people? or What issues are these people having to deal with? From this analysis performance measures can be extracted.

A number of examples are necessary to illustrate the variety of uses for content analysis. In an organisation whose main output was research reports we analysed *reports in various stages of completion*, following individual reports as they were initiated below and went up the hierarchy for eventual release. We found two unusual things. First, an enormous number of grammatical and syntactical errors. Second, a need (not always met) for the senior managers to edit well. Neither of these factors figured at that time in the performance appraisal; the first because it was not thought that research scientists would make mistakes in grammar and syntax, the second because nobody had thought of it.

On another occasion it was the *performance appraisal records* themselves which were content-analysed, in a firm where the appraisal system was under review. The forms allowed the managers to set objectives for the employee, so the first content analysis was a simple accumulation of all the objectives people set. Also, at the end of the appraisal forms managers were requested to make recommendations for training and development needs. These recommendations were analysed to discover the skills and abilities managers said their people needed. This was a particularly fruitful content analysis; not only was the system redesigned for closer resemblance to managers' requirements, but also the content analysis yielded much data that could be used in training and back-up information.

Rackham and Morgan[7] give an example of content analysis used to investigate the differences between successful and unsuccessful telephone salesgirls. They recorded the transactions (with permission, of course) and content-analysed them. Among a number of fascinating results, they show one which overturns the popular wisdom as preached on communications courses: the successful salesgirl was much more likely to exhibit 'continuity behaviour' during pauses caused by, say, her need to search through a timetable. By continuity behaviour Rackham and Morgan mean the *sotto voce* murmurings – 'ho hum, toodle-oo, let's see now ...' noises – which most communications courses tell people to suppress. Apparently on the telephone during long pauses such behaviour reassures the caller and reduces the likelihood that he will ring off before the sale has been made.

From these three examples of content analysis, taken from diverse fields, the reader can see its utility in the search for performance measures. Like critical incident, it is unlikely to tell you everything, because not everything that goes on is recorded, and different firms keep different kinds of records. A little ingenuity is often needed to find the right place to look. Content analysis has the great advantage that, while it is field research and not speculation, it does not involve the line managers who are being researched. One can lock oneself up with a bundle of files and discover a great deal of information, and no one need know. Often when an appraisal scheme is proposed the personnel department is expected to have it installed and running within three weeks of the managing director's agreement. (We have had at a two-day seminar someone who arrived with a blank sheet of paper and was expected to have his system designed by the end of the week!) Using content analysis the personnel department can do a good deal of sound research into performance criteria before putting their suggestions to the line; thus they can be seen to respond quickly.

Performance questionnaire

This is the most powerful, and the most time-consuming, of our three suggested methods for deriving criteria. Its end-product is a very detailed list of the characteristics which distinguish effective from ineffective performers in a given type of job, as effectiveness is presently perceived. Such a list is useful for many purposes besides design of the appraisal system; it may form the start of serious organisation development work, with distinct plans for measureable change; it may affect selection, promotion, counselling, and many other areas.

A performance questionnaire consists of a list of bipolar statements applicable to performance in the job under consideration (for example production manager, or salesman). A typical PQ would contain somewhere between 80 and 120 items, and an extract from one – used in analysing production managers – is given in Figure 3.1. Questionnaires are distributed to the *managers* of the job under consideration, or to *job-holders* themselves, or both. They are asked to think of the most effective performer in that job they have working for them (or work with) and to describe him, warts and all, by means of the questionnaire. The name of the performer must not, however, be given. Then a few weeks later the same questionnaire is distributed to the same people and they are asked to describe the least effective performer – again a real person, but anonymous. A simple statistical analysis is then performed to discover which items differentiate between effective and ineffective performance as it is presently viewed. It is also possible to derive a list of those characteristics strongly associated with effectiveness, and another list of those strongly associated with ineffectiveness, and to turn these into pen-pictures, as in Figure 3.2(a) and (b) which is the result of the full performance questionnaire (Figure 3.1).

1 2 3 4 5

		1 2 3 4 5	
1	He works best at his own pace.		He works best when other people or events set the pace.
2	He manages by means of group objectives.		He manages by means of individual objectives.
3	He encourages his people's best work only when he is certain of the project's success.		He encourages his people's best work at all times.
4	He draws up development plans for his people.		He does not draw up development plans for his people.
5	He cannot handle problems when the situation is ambiguous.		He can handle problems in an ambiguous situation.
6	He asks for help when he needs it.		He does not ask for assistance.
7	He prepares himself thoroughly to meet demanding situations.		He plays demanding situations off-the-cuff.
8	He can tolerate being disliked.		He cannot tolerate being disliked.
9	He asks 'how will this affect XYZ?'		He asks 'how will this affect my area?'
10	He lets his colleagues know when he has useful information for them.		He doesn't do so.
11	He announces decisions, without explanations.		He announces decisions and explains the reasons.
12	He can argue well to a departmental brief.		He cannot argue well to a departmental brief.
13	He is overawed by high status outsiders.		He is not overawed by high status outsiders.

Fig. 3.1   Performance questionnaire with list of bipolar statements.

		1	2	3	4	5	
14	He avoids doing unpleasant tasks.						He gets on with unpleasant tasks.
15	He acts as his own personnel officer.						He depends upon his personnel officer.
16	He is effective only in small groups.						The size of the group does not affect his effectiveness.
17	He confronts difficult issues.						He avoids dealing with difficult issues.
18	He makes sure he gets technical answers rights.						He makes sure he gets the commercial answers right.
19	He is less than honest under pressure.						He is honest under pressure.
20	He sees legislation as an opportunity.						He sees legislation as a threat.
21	He doesn't take work home.						He takes work home.

Fig. 3.1 (continued)

(a) *Effective manager*

1 *Handling, ambiguity and stress.* He can handle problems in an ambiguous situation, and can cope with situations where the company policy is not clear. He will bend the rules. Under pressure his performance improves *but* he stays honest. When delays and frustrations occur he can get on with other things. He prefers to set his own standards for his work, but he will give his best efforts no matter where the work originates.

2 *Scale of operations.* He plans several steps ahead, and he is more effective when handling the 'big picture' than the details. Once he has made a proposal he follows it through to make sure things happen, and he monitors the effect of change over time. He will take action even though the results will not be apparent

Fig. 3.2   Pen pictures, derived from completed performance questionnaires, showing the characteristics associated with (a) an effective and (b) an ineffective manager.

for some time. He plans in order to maximise his possible gains, not to minimise his possible losses.

3 *Concern for self development.* He has a development plan for himself. He sees himself as a manager. When he is in a rut he pulls himself out, and he asks for help when he needs it. He encourages new ideas and he learns from his mistakes.

4 *Problem diagnosis and solving.* He puts priorities on what needs to be done, and when he presents a problem he offers a solution. He takes action on causes rather than on symptoms. He can distinguish correctly between what he cannot and can control; between fact and opinion; and between negotiation and problem-solving situations.

5 *Tough-mindedness.* He confronts difficult issues; he puts a stop to wasteful projects on time, and he gets rid of poor performers. He judges people by end results, not by effort. He prepares himself thoroughly to meet demanding situations, and when he is in a conflict the other person backs down. He will use his authority when the situation demands it, and he is not overawed by high status outsiders. He listens to people even when he doesn't like what they have to say. He will travel anywhere, anytime, and he gets on with unpleasant tasks.

6 *Technical competence.* He has a good memory and his visual presentation of data is clear. He tries to understand other functions' jargon and he reads material of wide management interest. He considers safety matters as an integral part of production, and as a people problem as well as a technical problem. He acts as his own personnel officer.

7 *Relations with boss.* He passes information upwards when necessary, and he defends rather than blames his subordinates to his boss.

8 *Relations with colleagues.* He is more effective dealing with people than with paper. He lets his colleagues have any useful information he might have for them, and he will respond to informal requests for help; he checks to see if his decisions will affect others. He contacts people face-to-fact, and co-ordinates by getting people together rather than by one-to-one contact. He invites to meetings only the people who need be there, and the size of the group does not affect his effectiveness. On the telephone he keeps his impact. He argues well to a departmental brief.

Fig. 3.2 (continued)

9   *Company policy and priorities.* He keeps up-to-date on company priorities, and up-to-date on current affairs as they affect the company. He anticipates the effect of new legislation, and he sees unionisation as just another factor to be managed. He is concerned to present XYZ to the public in the best possible light.

10   *Management of Subordinates.* He allows his subordinates to consult him and he encourages them to talk to him directly. He passes information downwards when necessary and he tells his people what his job involves. He asks for their suggestions before making decisions; when he has to announce a decision he explains the reasons and strives to win his staff's acceptance rather than just saying 'those are the rules'. He will discuss his staff's personal problems if this affects their performance. He draws up development plans for his people and frequently tells them how they are performing. He assesses people's potential correctly, and his subordinates' performance improves over time. He encourages their best work at all times, not just when he is confident of success. He sets group objectives and he staffs to meet average, not peak, demands.

(b)   *Ineffective manager*

1   *Handling ambiguity and stress.* He cannot handle problems in an ambiguous situation, and he waits for company guidance before moving. He is more effective when dealing with a familiar problem, and when a crisis occurs he gives it all his attention rather than absorbing the workload. He avoids doing unpleasant things, and under greater than normal pressure his performance gets worse, but he remains honest. The presence of others makes him less decisive.

2   *Scale of operations.* He is most effective when working on the details rather than the big picture, and he plans one step at a time; his long term predictions are inaccurate. When he has made a proposal he assumes things will happen and he does not monitor the effect of change over time.

3   *Concern for self-preservation.* He avoids difficult issues and he goes by the rule book. He repeats his mistakes. He concentrates on enhancing his own effectiveness, rather than his boss's, and he asks how things will affect his area rather than how they affect XYZ. He cannot tolerate being disliked, and he listens to

Fig. 3.2 (continued)

people only to have his point of view confirmed. He sees himself as a manager rather than as a specialist, but he has no self development plans and if he gets into a rut he does not pull himself out.

4 *Problem diagnosis and solving.* He deals with each matter as it arises rather than assigning priorities. When he presents a problem he also offers a solution, but he takes action on symptoms of problems rather than causes. He plans to minimise his losses rather than to maximise his gains. He cannot distinguish between fact and opinion, nor between what he can and cannot control, nor between negotiating situations and problem solving situations.

5 *The timid hedgehog.* His in-tray is full, and he takes work home. He lets wasteful projects run on and he tolerates poor performers. In conflicts he's the one to back down. He does not ask for assistance, and he sees legislation as a threat. He judges people's performance by criteria other than profit. He is reluctant to use his own authority, though he is not overawed by high status outsiders. He will travel anywhere, any time.

6 *Technical competence.* He makes sure he gets the technical answers, rather than the commercial answers, right. His estimates of the time required to meet the task are incorrect, and he does not speak a foreign language.

7 *Relations with boss.* He gives top priority to the demands of senior management rather than to the customer or competitor, and he passes information upwards when necessary.

8 *Relations with colleagues.* He is more effective dealing with paperwork than with people. He assumes that people have understood him rather than checking this and he does not check the effect of his decisions on others. He will respond to informal requests for help. He co-ordinates by one-to-one contact rather than getting people together, and he cannot argue to a departmental brief. He must get himself involved in the work of less experienced specialists. He depends upon his personnel officer.

9 *Company policy and priorities.* His knowledge of company priorities is not up-to-date and he is not up-to-date on company-related current affairs. He sees unionisation as inhibiting his freedom to plan, and he is surprised by the effect of new legislation.

10 *Management of subordinates.* He will allow his sub-

Fig. 3.2 (continued)

ordinates to consult him, and he will discuss their personal problems with them if this affects their performance. He circulates reports to his staff and passes information downwards when necessary. Though he sets standards for his staff he does not tell them how they are performing and he does not draw up development plans for them. His assessment of his people's potential is incorrect, and he under-utilises them. His subordinates' performance improves over time, and one or more of them could take his place if necessary. He is not the sole ideas man in his section – ideas can arise anywhere – but if his people are in difficulties he takes on the job himself rather than helping them find their own way out. He puts over company decisions in terms of 'those are the rules' and he does not tell them what his job involves. He sees their job as providing a service to him, rather than his job to provide them with a service. He does not allow people to make précis for him, but reads everything himself.

Fig. 3.2 (continued)

This is a very large amount of data on the perceived characteristics of effectiveness, and its detail and specificity usually make it fascinating for line managers. The next step, however, is to ask whether one wishes to perpetuate the present picture or to change it. (It may be, for instance, that the effective manager is seen as much too 'nice' for changing market conditions, as was the case in the firm whose data we have used for our examples here.) The final picture is then interrogated to discover which of the performance measures should be used in the performance appraisal system.

The question may be asked: Where do the questions in the performance questionnaire come from? We have experimented with a number of sources. A conference of personnel experts is unlikely to produce a high-yielding questionnaire. Questionnaires based on line managers' concepts of their job are much more likely to succeed. (It goes without saying that there is no universal performance questionnaire; what is effective behaviour in one firm can be the reverse in another.) A satisfactory questionnaire is possible from critical incident interviews, but for an investigation in detail we recommend that the questions be derived from repertory grid interviews with job-holders.

The *Repertory Grid*[8] is a technique for interviewing and mapping someone's thought-processes. It derives originally from clinical psychology and has only recently been used in industry. One of its chief merits is that it combines intense thoroughness of interview with the minimum possible bias on the part of the interviewer. For the design of a performance questionnaire the interview procedure is taken only part of the way possible. The interviewer begins by asking the interviewee to write down on eight small cards the names of eight activities he performs in his job. The interviewer helps by asking trigger questions: 'Something you do which is important, something which takes up a lot of your time, something important but unlikely to appear in your diary, another important activity, another time-consuming one ...' and so on until eight activities are listed. (The names of customers or colleagues or products or projects could also be used if these are convenient.) Then the interviewer takes the cards three at a time, according to a prepared schedule, and hands them to the interviewee with the question: 'Can you tell me one way in which any two of these resemble each other and differ from the third?' The result will be a two-ended answer called a *construct* – for example the interviewee might say: 'Those two are at my own discretion but the other is under someone else's control,' giving the construct *under own control – under other's control.* After twenty or so triads the interviewer goes back to the beginning and asks the interviewee to specify which side of the construct is most important for him to do well, in order to be effective in his job. When he has made that judgement he is invited to say why, with the question: 'Would you like to tell me a little more about that?'. An hour to an hour and a half will probably produce between twenty and sixty constructs, which can be turned very easily into items for the performance questionnaire; up to twenty managers may be interviewed for material for the performance questionnaire.

This necessarily brief outline of the repertory grid and performance questionnaire technique is augmented by a much fuller discussion and practical guide in Stewart and Stewart *Tomorrow's Men Today* [9]. Some indication of the strength of the technique is the comparative yield of performance questionnaire with and without repertory grid: we find that PQs designed on the 'workshop' principle have somewhere between a 12 and a 20 per cent yield of items discriminating between effective and ineffective performers, while PQs designed from repertory grid interviews have a yield of between 67 and 85 per cent.

The choice between critical incident, content analysis, and performance questionnaire rests on a number of factors. Critical incident is a good technique for getting a lot of information quickly, perhaps enabling one to decide whether further research of a more thorough nature is required. A critical incident survey usually tells one something useful about the balance of priorities within the organisation, at the key point of 'where does it hurt most?' It is therefore useful whenever one suspects that there is an imbalance within the performance criteria – as with the engineers we mentioned earlier – or if it is proposed to transfer an appraisal system from one part of the firm to another. Critical incident also points up organisational blind spots. It is a useful tool in the hands of the researcher who is ignorant of the business area he is investigating, or who wishes to protect himself from preconceptions – all he has to do is listen. And it enables one to put costs on the incidents, which is another useful source of priorities and helps to get line managers' attention.

Content analysis is a slower process, more painstaking, and perhaps more thorough. Its great benefit is that it is non-reactive – there is no need to disturb busy people by interviews or questionnaires. It is freer from fakery than most interview or questionnaire techniques, as one is going over historical data. It enables one to get a feeling for priorities, and for the real nature of the business and the performance measures being applied – as in our example of the analysis of reports-in-progress, where no one would publicly admit to the need for training in grammar, and no one had insight enough to see the need for training in editing. The drawbacks of content analysis are: the length of time it can take; the fact that not all transactions are recorded, so that one has to search sometimes for data; and its historical nature, which is unhelpful if one is looking for performance measures in an entirely new area. With an existing appraisal system, however, we would always advise doing a content analysis of appraisal forms to see what standards managers really are using.

Performance questionnaire is the most thorough of the techniques we suggest, but has the highest yield and the greatest likelihood of spin-off benefits into other areas (e.g. selection, assessment of potential, and organisation development work). When the health of the whole organisation is under question, or major changes have happened or are foreseen, then performance questionnaire is worthwhile. It is also useful if sensitivity to the organisation's 'culture' is required for some reason – a recent history of takeovers or mergers, after which there is an increased need to apply common performance standards to the component parts and to be seen to be doing so.

All the techniques we have illustrated, and performance questionnaire in particular, yield a list of skills, characteristics, etc., which the research has shown to be important in the eyes of the managers doing the job. This list is only descriptive, not prescriptive. It should be followed by detailed interrogation of senior managers and directors to discover whether they think these characteristics should be perpetuated or some other ones sought. It is difficult not to over-emphasise the importance of this procedure, and the effect it has on the senior managers concerned; eighteen hours, spread over some months, going through the detailed implications of a performance questionnaire, is the time taken by one managing director, with significant business improvements to follow.

At the end of the research, the researcher has a long list of characteristics, or objectives, or both. He has to translate them into useful compact labels for the appraisal form. In doing this it is inevitable that some of the detail will be lost; a detailed description of good decision-making condenses to one or two words. But the detail should never be lost sight of; the full descriptions of characteristics should be used in training, and should form part of the appraisal guidance literature to appraisers and appraisees.

Putting performance measures on paper

A number of options are open here. On the one hand, performance measures can be set for the individual appraisee by the manager, in the form of specific, job-related objectives. On the other hand, a list of measures can be provided on the form for the manager to measure the appraisee on. Often the two are combined.

Setting individual objectives

Management by Objectives (MbO) was described in some detail in Chapter One. In some firms MbO and performance appraisal are synonymous. In classical MbO the chief executive begins by considering deeply the business he is in, the targets he wishes to achieve in the next twelve months or so (probably taking into account a rolling five-year plan), and any constraints or problems which might hamper the achievement of these targets. It is crucial that he specify the targets clearly so that he and others will be in no doubt when they are achieved. Then he meets with the people who report to him, and assigns to them their own targets so that the sum of the targets equals his own. Each person discusses his own targets, makes plans for meeting and overcoming difficulties, and in the process absorbs commitment to the goals of the organisation. The procedure is repeated further down the line.

Performance appraisal has in common with MbO the reviewing of past performance and planning for the future by setting identifiable goals. But performance appraisal is not dependent upon the downward systematic flow of information from top management. In MbO a manager must not set objectives until his own have been set. He will probably do a better performance appraisal if he himself has been appraised, but he can, and sometimes must, do an appraisal interview when his own appraisal is two years overdue.

The best way to set individual objectives is to limit the number – no more than six, say – and with this number cover the key result areas of the employee's job. Setting objectives in a performance appraisal is *not* the same as writing a job description; complete coverage is not the aim. If this is not made clear managers will wear themselves out setting huge numbers of 'objectives' (the record stands at 181) and employees may refuse to do things that are not listed in their objectives. Guidance on the appropriate key result areas comes, if needed, from the research on performance measures earlier. The freedom managers have to name their own objectives varies from firm to firm; in some jobs, e.g. sales, target-setting is so much a natural part of the business that assistance is not required. There are other jobs where it is much more difficult to set objectives and here managers may need assistance. This can be provided by naming the key result areas on the appraisal form but leaving to manager's discretion the framing of the actual objective; or by supplying managers with a 'shopping-basket' of objectives from which to select. This works best when the shopping-basket contains an overwhelming number of examples; give them a few only and some will not bother to choose.

People have difficulties defining the term *objective*. In one firm whose appraisal system was ten years old we asked groups of managers to define the term, and got varied and often conflicting responses. Personnel jargon multiplies here, as people add concepts like *aim, target, goal, purpose*, etc., with subtle but idiosyncratic variations in meaning. We offer the following definition as used in performance appraisal: 'An *objective* is a statement of what has to be done, the purpose for which it is to be done, with measures for the achievement of both of these'.

Thus a good example of an objective is: 'Prepare a summary of the services available to assist redundant managers, ready by mid-June, so that the redundancies planned for next year are smoothly handled. Measures: minimum financial cost to company, maximum financial benefit to individuals, no industrial relations problems, managers seeking new jobs get them in four months, no good people leave from fear, and exit interviews show less bitterness than last time.' The person given this objective knows what he has to do, why, and can tell if he has done it well. Because he knows the *purpose* he will not slavishly follow the first part of the remit; if during his search he encounters a company desperately anxious to recruit managers of the kind his firm is making redundant, he will not dismiss this information with, 'My job's to do this survey, I don't know what it's used for'.

Some managers have difficulty setting objectives because they believe that something can only be an objective if it is numerically measurable. Outside the simpler sales and production functions they are lost. It is important to stress that an objective must be achievable, and one must be able to tell when one has achieved it, but that this judgement need not be numerical. The bitterness of exit interviews can be judged by an impartial judge; he will not put numbers on the bitterness, and he may admit to an element of subjectivity in the way he makes the judgement. As long as he can make the subjectivity explicit, so that another person would have no trouble in 'borrowing' his frame of reference, then he is still engaged in objective-setting.

The objective-setting procedure has a number of advantages. It makes employee and manager look at the specific needs of the job. They set specific, personal targets, so the commitment from the employee is likely to be higher. During the review of the last year's performance reference to the original objectives is helpful in pulling their concentration away from recent events so that they review the whole year. Where there is management by objectives to any degree, the manager can reveal his own objectives and show how the employee's objectives fit in. And the concentration on finding success measures for each objective helps the employee in monitoring and controlling his own performance later. Among the disadvantages of objective-setting are its mechanistic, over-numerical approach in the wrong hands; the possibility that objectives will be seen as limiting freedom; and difficulties that arise when a system is taken from one part of the organisation and applied to another.

Rating scales, narrative summaries

Most appraisal forms contain one rating scale at least – an over-all summary of performance, probably on a five-point scale from excellent to unsatisfactory. The appraisal form of Cloud, Cuckoo & Partners, discussed in the previous chapter, con-tains a great many such rating scales, mostly of personality rather than performance.

As opposed to objectives, which are agreed individually, these ratings are imposed on the manager by their presence on the form. Everyone affected by the appraisal form is judged on these provided criteria. This is why we laid heavy emphasis earlier in this chapter on the need to get the criteria *right*. The provision of labels invites the development of five-, seven-, or even nine-point scales; these invite computerisation and feeding into complex personnel record systems, leading to meaningless precision which will not be abandoned, because it was expensive to set up.

Managers can be asked to rate employees on company-wide criteria without making these criteria into rating scales. In some firms the appraisal form contains a series of prompting words – accuracy, speed, cash control – and the manager has to write two sentences summarising the employee's performance on each label. 'We used to make them rate on a five-point scale,' said the personnel executive in one such firm, 'but we felt that in head office we were losing touch with them as people, so we changed to the keyword system.' Senior management desire a family feel-ing throughout and this is one way they express these priorities.

Most firms using company-wide labels show a wish to turn them into scales. There is no point in using a scale bigger than five-point; the average adult is at his limit of discrimination on a seven-point scale, so forcing him to use one will cause unsyste-matic inaccuracies. However, given a five-point scale there are always some managers who create their own categories: A–, B+, and so on. As long as their number is manageable, don't worry.

The design of rating scales is something that nobody ever gets completely right, because of conflicting demands and expectations. A good first attempt, though, is to supply a five-point scale like this:

A	B	C	D
Exceeds in all respects	Exceeds in most respects	Exceeds in some respects	Meets basic requirements

	E		
	Fails to meet basic requirements		

This gives four grades of satisfactory performer and one grade of poor performer. A satisfactory performer who is just meeting requirements will be graded D. He may feel that if he is a satisfactory performer he should be graded C, because C fits half-way along the scale. However, it is less trouble explaining to D performers that they *are* meeting requirements than it is to make and justify differentiations between grades of unsatisfactory performers, which would be the consequence of grading Ds as Cs. Managers who use this scale will inevitably let their ratings creep up towards the top end, and occasional re-education will be necessary; as we said, no system is perfect. The advantage of the scale given above – and it is an advantage that can be transferred to other scales – is that it does not use the word *average*. This word brings instant confusion to rating scales, for two reasons.

First, it is imprecise. In an ordinary, growing firm most people will be rated somewhere between B and C; given a certain amount of upward drift, there may even be a peak at B. One could then say that B performers were 'average'. Or, going on blind logic and a five-point scale, one could say that C was the average, because it was the mid-point. Then there is an argument for saying that D is defined as an average, basically satisfactory performance. Chaos and an unresolvable argument ensue, with further piquancy if it pleases you to distinguish between mean, median, and mode.

Second, to say that someone is an average performer is implicitly comparing him with the people around him, and this way lies trouble also. Once the appraisal system allows people to be rated on how they compare with each other, endless arguments about fairness and opportunity result. Compare the man with the basic requirements of the job, and you are using a more stable yardstick.

It is possible to use other labels for the points on the scale, perhaps reflecting the content of the particular scale and bringing in some of the detail from research on the performance characteristics. However our caution about the use of the word *average* remains valid.

In comparison with individual objectives, rating scales exhibit a different set of advantages. They apply the same yardstick to many different employees, thus allowing the company to audit its talent. They make comparisons easier, whether between two people considered for promotion or one person judged now and compared with two years ago. They are rather less vulnerable to abuse from managers who won't or can't understand the system, and they are easy to apply in areas where objective-setting is difficult. Most appraisal systems therefore combine the two; an objective-setting exercise, an overall rating, and ratings on specific scales.

Case study: Management by Objectives in the service division

We have emphasised in this chapter the need to base performance measures, whether they be objectives or rating scales, on empirical research. As an example of how things can go badly awry when this does not happen, consider the case of a firm where a Management by Objectives scheme, which had worked well in the sales division, was installed wholesale in the division which services sales' equipment. No thought had been given to the type of objective people should set; instructions were as for sales, with the man at the top identifying objectives and constraints and passing them down.

Top management, moving in exalted circles, complied. Middle management were not informed about the system nor was their commitment gained. The problem presented itself as howls of anguish from first-line managers who were expected to do appraisals but could not see the point.

On investigation it was found that the most important of the head manager's objectives was not to overspend his budget. The constraints on this were the minimum amount of service he could offer customers. His life was spent budgeting, planning, thinking of ways of increasing productivity. Examination of the first-line managers' job showed entirely the opposite. They were in business to give service, and the constraint on them was how much money they could spend. When the objective-setting had been done, the top manager had divided his budget between the managers reporting into him and had them given each one budgetary objectives. They had done this with their people, and so on down to first-line manager; however, middle managers had not noticed the incongruity of their actions because no one was pressing them. For industrial relations reasons the first-line managers were pressed to do appraisals. They looked at their own 'objectives' in disbelief – cut overtime, cut travel time, closer monitoring of expenses . . . These were not the key result areas of their jobs! Nor could they take these objectives and slice them further to fit the service engineers themselves; the engineers would want to talk about customers and machines and stores and parts. So they cried for help.

What we see here is a genuine reversal between objectives and constraints as we travel from top to bottom of the organisation, and an appraisal/MbO system installed with no sensitivity to the presence of this reversal. A little research prior to the installation of the system would have revealed this – critical incident clearly reveals such changes in priorities, for example. The crucial role of middle managers would then have been apparent, and their aid enlisted instead of their being ignored. Sample objectives, or guidance on the kinds of objectives appropriate at each level, could have been provided. As it was, the problem took a long time to detect and diagnose, so that the whole appraisal system had been brought into disrepute by the time a solution was proposed. And all for the want of a little research on performance criteria.

Summary

The need to base performance criteria on empirical research into the real needs for success in the job cannot be over-emphasised. Measures, whether individual objectives or company-wide scales, should relate to performance rather than personality. Research methods include: discussion with employee groups; critical incident method; content analysis; performance questionnaire.

When measures are translated into objectives, guidance for managers in certain areas may be necessary, though their responsibility for setting individual objectives should not be removed. When measures are translated into rating scales, no more than five points on the scale should be used (if points are to be assigned at all) and the use of the word 'average' when labelling these points should be avoided at all costs. Idiosyncracies in the use of scales, and drift towards the top of the scale, are to be expected; remedial action depends upon the purposes for which the scales are used.

4 Installing a system: system design

Though appraisal systems begin with the need for employee and manager systematically to review the previous year's work and to plan for the next year, most appraisal systems do not stop there. They generate data which other parts of the firm could find useful – about business objectives, training needs, salary planning, and so on. Also, the introduction of an appraisal system where there was none before is an intervention into the management style of the firm; there is the opportunity to move towards a more participative style of management, the opportunity to encourage managers to delegate more, the opportunity to monitor employee feelings and attitudes. In particular, changes in style among middle managers – who both do appraisals and are appraised – are likely to result from a new or changed appraisal scheme.

The spin-off benefits from appraisal are one reason for giving close consideration to the actual shape of the appraisal system. Another reason is that historically most appraisal systems have either developed like Topsy – they just growed, aided perhaps by pictures of other people's appraisal systems – or they were purchased intact from a consultant, or taken over after an acquisition. Systems developed in this way stand a good chance of being ignored or falling into disrepute, or of collecting vast quantities of useless information. It is for this reason that we devote most of this chapter to considering the four parties to appraisal: the appraisee, the appraiser, the central planning and control functions, and outside bodies. Each of these parties has an interest in the appraisal process; each has purposes which could be served by the appraisal system, depending upon the form the system takes. For example, if it is required that the appraisee contributes towards the appraisal process, then some implications are immediately obvious: he must know about the appraisal, he must probably take part in an interview, and perhaps there should be attempts to get him to prepare himself beforehand. If it is intended to relate salary planning to the appraisal process, then the appraisal system must contain performance ratings, based on a clearly identified scale or scales.

We suggest that the reader who is contemplating designing a

system should follow the chart given as Figure 4.1, selecting for himself those aspects which are most important for his purposes. The implications for system design are set out in the chart and the text. Simplicity is the keynote, at least to begin with; try not to overload the system, especially with purposes which belong to the last two parties. The reader who already has a system should compare the features of his system with those on the chart, and ask whether particular features are necessary or could be improved. The chart is probably an over-simplification but it is a better starting-point than borrowing someone else's system and trying to make it fit.

PARTY TO APPRAISAL	PURPOSES	IMPLICATIONS FOR SYSTEM DESIGN
APPRAISEE	Contribution to the appraisal process	Appraisal by face-to-face interview
	Acceptance of appraiser's evaluation	Appraisee must sign form at end of interview
	Opportunity for long term guidance	Planning or objective-setting for the future; discussion of ambitions; discussion of training needs; discussion of abilities in general
	Use of appraisal for self-development	Setting goals in interview; use of preparation for counselling form; retention of written objectives; mini-appraisals through the year
APPRAISER	Employee working to agreed goals	Setting and recording objectives or personal goals
	Co-ordination of employees' goals	Timing of appraisals from top of organisation downwards; minimised time-lag between appraisals at top and bottom; co-ordination and control of appraisals from centre

Fig. 4.1   Appraisal purposes and system design

APPRAISER	Coaching the employee	Setting specific performance targets; employee suggests targets and/or measures; both parties keep records and use for regular, frequent review
	Listening to the employee	Appraisee uses preparation for counselling form; appraiser records employee's comments on appraisal form separately from or integrated with his review of performance
	Early detection of problems	Use of general, open-ended questions — aspirations, unused skills, constraints on performance, etc.; use of preparation for counselling form; grandfather sign-off of appraisal form before interview
	Equity between subordinates	Use of common performance measures on all appraisees; grandfather sign-off of appraisals before or after; management information system programmed to detect broken trends or unusual patterns
	Training of subordinates	Record of training needs
	Use of money as compensation	Give salary increase at the appraisal interview
	Use of money as incentive	Forbid mention of salary increase at appraisal interview
	Manpower skills audit	Use of common performance criteria across employees; central collation of measures on these criteria
	Manpower forecasting	Enter employee's measures on required characteristics (age, job history, mobility, family circumstances, etc.) on appraisal form

Fig. 4.1   (continued)

CENTRAL PLANNING AND CONTROL	Assessment of employee potential	Manager rates employee on scale of perceived promotability; manager rates employee on appropriate performance criteria; discussion of employee ambitions; central collation of these records
	Succession planning	Manager rates employee's suitability for named job(s); discussion of employee ambitions; central collation of records
	Salary planning	Manager gives overall rating of performance; central collating with or without intervention to produce conformity to agreed norm
	Training planning	Record of training needs
	Equity between subordinates	Define and communicate scope of scheme; grandfather checks appraisal ratings; central monitoring of quality and quantity; grievance procedure
	Downward transmission of company objectives	Centrally co-ordinated order and timing of appraisals
	Problem and grievance detection and handling	Employee sign-off of form; employee comments on form; grandfather or personnel intervention on critical forms; discussion of employee's unused skills, constraints on action, etc.
OUTSIDE PARTIES	Industry Training Board's requirements	Consult ITB documents and staff for advice and guidance
	Codes of good practice	Ensure performance criteria are relevant to job; ensure that no group of employees gets special treatment; give the appropriate guidance on use of appraisals with poor performers

Fig. 4.1   (continued)

OUTSIDE PARTIES	Pay restraint	Clear communication to both parties of restrictions on manager's discretion; emphasis on remaining motivational use of appraisal system
	Privacy restrictions	Record forms designed so employee can see whole form; guard against misleading interpretations; employee sign-off or comments; grievance procedure available; policy on who has access to appraisal data

Fig.4.1 (continued)

The appraisee's purposes

Contribution to the appraisal process is obtained by the appraisal taking the form of a face-to-face interview between appraiser and appraisee. The contribution is likely to be increased if the system's publicity makes it clear that a minimum length of time – say half an hour – is to be spent on the appraisal. Employees can be encouraged to take a significant part in the interview by training managers to begin the interview with questions rather than evaluations, and partly by the use of a preparation for counselling form which the appraisee uses before the interview to structure his thoughts about his past performance, future goals, etc.

Acceptance of appraiser's evaluation cannot, of course, be guaranteed in all cases, but if the appraisee is required to sign that he has taken part in the appraisal, or has seen the form, and is in agreement with its contents, then the likelihood that the appraiser will strive for acceptance is increased and the possibility of action elsewhere to follow up disagreements is opened.

Opportunity for long term guidance of the employee is increased by any provision for discussion of the future: setting goals or objectives for the next year, recording the appraisee's ambitions, discussions of his abilities in general, discussion of training needs, etc. The distinction between setting objectives one year ahead, and discussing the employee's abilities without specific reference to the job in hand, is important. If the latter

course is adopted decisions must be taken about whether counselling is to take into account the current and predicted job market.
Also, appraising managers should beware of appearing to
promise the appraisee a job.

Use of appraisal for self-development is facilitated by setting
personal goals during the appraisal interview. An even greater
likelihood is produced by the use of preparation for counselling
forms. If the goals are largely predetermined by the technology
of the organisation or by a Management by Objectives programme, additional discretion should be given to the employee
in the derivation of success measures for these goals, and opportunity for setting one or two personal goals should be provided.
Copies of the appraisal records – at least those parts referring to
the objectives – should remain with the appraisee and manager,
and the possibility of mini-appraisals on a more than annual
frequency should be allowed for.

The manager's purposes

Employee working to agreed goals is brought about by setting
goals or objectives in the interview and recording them. The number and format of the goals may vary, according to the presence
of a Management by Objectives scheme. Where performance is
rated on a series of scales only, much more difficulty will be experienced in getting employees working towards specific goals,
especially when the quality of the performance is to change for
some reason – a new job, poor performance to be improved, etc.

Co-ordination of employees' goals requires the timing of
appraisal interviews to be systematised. For example, in a system
where objectives are to be passed from top to bottom there will
be a distinct appraisal cycle, starting with the top man and going
as rapidly as possible to the bottom. This will require a good deal
of co-ordination from the centre. It will also require that the
centre be powerful enough to insist that a dilatory manager does
his appraisals, and the risk that his appraisals will be done with a
bad grace has to be accepted. Guidance on the kinds of objectives
appropriate may be needed in staff groups or at middle manager
level in particular. In large firms the rapid transmission of objectives from top to bottom may not be possible without concentrating a lot of time on appraisal for a few weeks in the year, after
which appraisals are not performed. This can be distracting.

However, it is not necessary for there to be full co-ordination of objectives from top to bottom in order for the individual manager to set objectives that weld his team more closely.

Coaching the employee for better results throughout the year is achieved by setting specific performance improvement targets, with associated measures which the subordinate can use himself. A commitment for action from the appraising manager can also be recorded during the interview. Records of the appraisal are kept by employee and manager, and for intensive coaching purposes they are used for performance review at weekly or monthly intervals. For the sake of preservation of important documents, as well as to safeguard privacy, it is better if the records of improvement targets and measures are kept on a separate sheet from the rest of the appraisal record.

Listening to the employee and maybe modifying his own views as a result of what the appraisee has to say is, like any other skilled behaviour, difficult to design into a system. However, appraising managers are more likely to listen attentively if the subordinate has had a preparation for counselling form, as this will have filled him with ideas to talk about; similarly if the manager has to wait until after the interview has commenced before writing a summary of the employee's performance he may pay attention to the employee. The manager may fill in the performance record before the interview, but add the employee's views during the interview in a space provided; or he may rough out his performance review but not write it down until the employee has had a chance to discuss it. Space on the appraisal form for the employee's comments will also make the manager more attentive.

Early detection of problems is encouraged by questions that are not tied specifically to the job in hand over the last year and the next. Questions that encourage the employee to talk about his career aspirations, for example; or that ask if he has any unused skills or abilities; or that ask if he detects anything standing in the way of a better performance on his part or that of the organisation as a whole. Again, preparation for counselling forms help to concentrate the employee's mind on this. So does a provision that the appraising manager should see his own manager before the appraisal, either by mentioning the impending appraisal during regular meetings or by sending his manager the half-completed appraisal form before the interview. In either case the manager's manager may be able to warn the appraiser of potential difficulties. Managers must show discretion in the way information on problems is recorded; they must not take notes while the employee is explaining a problem, for instance, and perhaps should be warned to record *actions* on problems, not the problems themselves.

Equity between subordinates will probably never be completely achieved. The application of common performance measures to all subordinates encourages thinking about equity; if each appraisee has performance measures exclusive to him, then comparisons are difficult. Discretion in striking out performance measures must be given to appraising managers. The grandfather figure's help in preserving equity is enlisted by allowing him to see the appraisal records of the managers under him, so that he signs the form before the appraisal, after the appraisal, or at both times. Sophisticated personnel records systems sometimes have built into them a process which compares the new performance rating with that person's previous ratings and initiates an exception report when the trend is broken. Opinions are divided about both the sensitivity and the practicality of this approach.

Training of subordinates is facilitated by the manager's filling in of a space recording training needs. Two cautions must be given here. First, a policy decision is needed about whether it will be the manager's responsibility to organise such training, or whether a central person will read all the appraisal records and take responsibility for the training. Central functions may monitor the records to assess trends in training needs without undertaking to arrange training for individual people. Second, it is possible to record training needs in at least two ways: by stating the skill that is deficient, or by naming a specific training course. If managers take the latter course, then it is worth while periodically checking their reasoning.

Use of money as compensation by the appraising manager allows for his using the appraisal interview to award a salary increase. After the discussion of performance, and an agreement about the performance rating, the manager names the salary increase (assuming outside factors allow this) before going on to plan for the future. Where money is used primarily for compensation, salary increases are usually given at regular intervals, perhaps according to a known set of invariant criteria. It should be made clear to employees that the appraisal interview will also cover a discussion of salary, and the point in the interview at which discussion can be expected – otherwise they will spend the interview until the mention of salary increases in inattentive expectancy.

Use of money as incentive by the appraising manager implies that the manager must have discretion about how much he gives, and when. The surprise value of an increase given a little earlier than expected, or a little more than expected, and its effect on performance and morale, is out of all proportion to the absolute size of the discrepancy; similarly the demoralising value of an increase delayed a little, or slightly less than expected, can be unexpectedly large. For the manager to use money as incentive he must be able to choose, within limits, how much he gives and when the news is broken; and it is therefore better if the performance appraisal interview is known by all parties to contain no reference to salary increases.

Central planning and control purposes

Manpower skills audits involve a centrally-conducted summary of the performance ratings of employees, divided into groups as appropriate. This implies that a common set of performance criteria must be applied to all employees, or that grouping of employees under particular sets of criteria appropriate to their job takes place. The number of criteria can be as small as one overall measure, or very large. The measure can be given on a rating scale or by narrative summaries which are manually condensed for inclusion in central records. Rating scales carry with them a temptation to computerise to excess; temptations to provide more ratings than people can sensibly use, or to take arithmetic averages across rating scales or across people, should be strongly resisted.

Manpower forecasting in various guises is helped by data taken from the appraisal records. Characteristics of the labour force can be extracted and examined – to produce age distributions, retirement forecasts, sickness and absence patterns, geographical mobility, talent drain indices, and so on. For these purposes demographic and other questions are included on the appraisal form. Before asking for the appraisal form to repeat information that is stored elsewhere in personnel records, such as age and job history, there should be a very strong case for taking these data from appraisal records rather than existing stock. The presence of much demographic data can be an intrusion on an appraisal form. When the normal demands are kept to a minimum, special requests for manpower planning information can be sent out with appraisal forms – with the equal treatment of women in the labour force many employers find that they need more information in order to plan pensions and other benefits schemes, for example.

Assessment of employee potential requires that the appraising manager form a judgement about the employee's future performance from consideration of his past and present performance. Most firms equate the assessment of potential with assessment of promotability, but this needs to be made clear. Several methods are used: for example, a time-scale on which the manager rates the employee's readiness for the next promotion; a scale on which the manager rates the employee's ultimate potential; or a series of performance criteria, which may include some not particularly relevant to the present job, on which present performance is rated for future matching with the known requirements of the next job. This information is collated centrally and may be used to prepare lists of employees of given potential. The lists are then brought out when a vacancy occurs. They can also form the basis of special training and development programmes for high-flyers or remedial groups.

Succession planning is the obverse of the assessment of potential. The appraising manager is asked to judge the employee's suitability, now or in the future, for a named job or jobs. This information is collated and used, perhaps in conjunction with geographical or job history data, to prepare a list of possible successors for positions down to a certain level in the organisation. Sophisticated systems allow one to record a planned successor, a 'calamity' successor, and a long-shot successor.

Salary planning information is taken from overall performance ratings, if these are given. Salary planning information is of two kinds: general and specific. In the *general* case, performance ratings are scrutinised for the organisation as a whole or in parts to allow general trends to be detected – if one division is being more generous than another, for example. Deviations from the desired norm are then treated at policy level. In the *specific* case the performance rating is translated directly into money terms for the employee, with no opportunity for adjustment between appraisal interview and salary increase. Here the control over individual managers is expressed as a limit to the number of high or low performance ratings they can give without getting special sanction. Given the tendency of performance ratings in all organisations to creep upwards over time, and the probable preference for a normal distribution amongst salary planners, there are two ways of reconciling the two. Either individual managers must be forced to make their ratings conform to a normal distribution over the year, or managers are given a little more latitude with performance ratings, the performance ratings are not tied rigidly to salary increases, and there is a periodic re-shuffle of the appraisal system as new performance criteria – with new expected distributions – are brought in.

Training planning requires that appraising managers record training needs, or a training plan, on the appraisal record. This is used to set priorities for training in the next year, and can also be used as the means whereby the appraisee is booked onto a training course if this is to be a central task rather than the manager's responsibility.

Equity between subordinates requires a number of actions. The scope of the appraisal system must be defined – all employees or some only – and provision made for highlighting delinquent managers. Grandfather figures are enlisted to maintain equity between their appraising managers, or where this is not possible then a substitute grandfather is found. Regular checks are made of the quantity and quality of appraisals, by random sampling amongst appraisal records and/or by employee attitude surveys. Employees thought to be especially at risk – moderate performers, those due for retirement, middle managers, people in small back rooms – may need special checks from time to time. Where performance criteria are not all appropriate for a given individual the appraisal form should allow this to be indicated. Assistance to employees to prepare themselves for the interview – by preparation for counselling forms or by discussion with a sympathetic outsider (someone from the personnel department, or a union officer) – helps reduce the apparent advantage which the verbally fluent have in interviews. And a clear system for airing grievances during or after the interview, which implies that the employee sees his rating and has to sign off the form indicating whether or not he is satisfied, also helps maintain equity of treatment.

Downward transmission of company objectives carries the clear implication that the appraisal include objective-setting and that these objectives start at the top and are shared and altered as they reach the bottom. The implications this carries for system design have been treated earlier in this chapter; however it is worth emphasising that the downward transmission of objectives can be initiated anywhere within the organisation if this is appropriate. In some organisations local management-by-objectives systems have been started by middle managers. These systems flourish as long as they meet the managers' purposes, and they usually attract a higher degree of commitment than centrally-imposed systems. Local variations in paperwork and timing may occur, and in most cases this should cause no concern at all to the central planning and control functions.

Problem and grievance detection and handling. Employee grievances are brought to light when the employee has to sign the form; when he can record his comments and/or disagreements; and when there is a system for referring back these disagreements to grandfather or to personnel. For this to work it must be clearly understood that the appraisal is not concluded until the employee is prepared to sign a document with which he is satisfied. Alternatively, no sign-off by the employee is required and the manager must write up an account of the interview, after which it is the responsibility of grandfather or of the personnel department to detect that a grievance exists and to initiate action. The training method given in the last part of Chapter Five is, on past evidence, likely to lead to a reduction in employee grievances remaining after the interview. Other trouble-spots besides overt grievances may also be sought; if unused employee skills are recorded, for instance, or suggestions to make the company a better place to work. Detailed analysis of performance against objectives may reveal problems with particular equipment, or procedures, or customers, which could then be examined in other ways.

Outside parties' purposes

Industry Training Boards often lay down conditions which an appraisal system must meet if exemption in this area is to be granted. Not surprisingly, they are also available to advise on system design to meet these conditions.

Codes of good practice imposed by various types of employment legislation affect system design. Though the subtleties of different codes may vary as the legislation changes, it is generally

safe to say that the appraisal system can be used to give warning
of unsatisfactory performance, and repeated special appraisals
satisfy the need for further warnings or records of improvement.
Any particular system, though, should probably be checked with
the appropriate agency. Performance ratings should be based on
criteria that can be shown to be related to success in the job, the
better to protect oneself from allegations of unfair discrimination on grounds of race or sex. A further safeguard is to ensure
that performance ratings are given against the job description
and not against other performers. It is unwise to specify performance criteria only for certain groups or individuals if these people
are at special risk of dismissal; it is similarly unwise to allow the
appraisal system to degenerate so that only poor performers, or
poor performers and high flyers, are appraised. These actions
could be construed as special treatment, and unfair.

Pay restraint has mighty implications for management and
motivation in general; it is worth emphasising that in periods of
pay restraint where managers' discretion over the amount, and
perhaps the frequency, of pay rises is limited, there is even more
need to carry out good performance appraisals although
managers may find them difficult. Neither does the removal of
pay restraint eliminate the need for more subtle examination of
why and how the employee performed.

Privacy restrictions already operate in the United States and in
some parts of Europe, giving the employee access as of right to
any data that the company may have about him. Legislation to
this end may well come soon in the UK. The implications for the
design of performance appraisal systems are many. With open
records managers must expect more contribution from the
appraisee during the interview. Their commitment to the system
and its purposes must be high. A system for handling grievances
must be designed well in advance of the first grievance and publicised. And in the part of the record form where the manager
records ambitions and/or potential, care must be taken to see that
this does not appear to be the promise of a job. In practice this
implies that simple scales asking 'When will he be ready for his
next promotion?' should not be used. Privacy laws will bring into
focus, for organisations previously undecided, the problem of
who else has access to appraisal data. Obviously the employee,
his manager, grandfather, and one or two in personnel or planning departments; but a decision must also be taken about
whether an appointing manager can trawl through appraisal

records looking for someone to interview, for example, and whether trade union officials should share that privilege.

With the aid of the chart an appraisal system, and much of the appraisal form, can be designed with reference to a specific set of purposes for the appraisal system. Much trouble later, in monitoring and controlling the system, is avoided by basing the design of the system on known purposes. Re-design of existing systems also becomes easier. Confusion sometimes arises when major changes affect the appraisal system; for example, in one organisation moving from merit payments to annual increments there came from managers the cry 'Now we can scrap the appraisal system!' Interestingly, the union involved wanted to maintain the system and said so firmly. This very clear clash of objectives was dealt with by going back to the original purposes of the appraisal system and reminding managers that salary administration was only a small part of the reason for appraisals. The job of conflict resolution would have been much more difficult without a clear statement of what the appraisal system was there to do.

Designing the form

What is included on the form depends upon the system; it would be wrong to prescribe a standard form here. General guidelines exist, though, as follows.

Most forms are a single sheet of paper folded to present four sides. Eight sides are probably the maximum tolerable. The outside should not contain sensitive information – basic demographic information only. Inside, it is best to progress from past to present to future. Last year's objectives, and whether they were reached; an overall rating of performance; rating of performance on individual rating scales, and narrative summaries of performance on given criteria; any special achievements or difficulties not recorded previously – all these, or a selection as appropriate, in whatever order seems logical, at the beginning of the form. If objectives are written on a separate sheet they should not, of course, be copied out again. It is unwise to ask the manager to make an overall rating of performance early in the completion of the form; this may wash over into more specific ratings if he has to make them. Rating scales should be clearly set

out, on no more than a five-point scale; a box provided for the
manager to indicate if this scale is not applicable, and perhaps
another box to indicate how important the quality being rated is
in the job being done. Ideally the polarity of the scales should be
randomised if a series of rating scales is used – the 'good' end of
the scale should not fall always at the left-hand side of the paper,
otherwise managers in a hurry will go down the paper ticking
automatically.

The records of past performances may occupy a single side,
or spread onto several sides. Allow plenty of space for writing
additional   comments,   and   separate   different   parts   of   the
records – leave a clear space between overall performance rating
and the preceding scale, for instance.

Logically the form moves on to a record of present performance, if this is to be included. An overall rating given to performance in the last six weeks, for example, with opportunity to write
down the reason should this deviate from the year-back look.

Next the records move to plans for the future. If individual
objectives are set, one or two pages divided down the middle with
Objectives recorded on the left and *Standard of Performance*
recorded on the right allow thorough recording of what has to be
done and how well. These should perhaps be on a removable
sheet of paper so that copies can be taken and retained. An
appraisal system less closely tied to objectives in the MbO sense
could give space on the form for recording individual goals in a
more narrative form.

Space now remains for a more general look to the future, in
whatever form is deemed appropriate. The items for inclusion,
and the way they are recorded, depend very much on whether the
employee is permitted to see the whole appraisal record. If he is
permitted to see everything, then anything which can be construed as an offer of a specific job must be avoided. So must any
question whereby the manager could be thought to state that the
employee had no potential left, or no future in the company. This
is not a very sensible question to ask anyway – how on earth can
anyone say to someone else that they have nothing left to
give? – but over-mechanistically framed questions sometimes
invite such an answer.

On the forward-looking part of the form go questions about
training, for the present or future jobs; special developmental
experiences other than training; ambitions the employee would
like to fulfil; suggestions he may have for improving the company in general; skills he feels are presently unused; any require-

ments he has for specialist career counselling, and so on. The manager may also be asked to record his opinion of the employee's potential; as stated elsewhere, there are difficulties in showing this rating to the employee if it consists of a single time-scale along which promotability is assessed, but fewer difficulties if the manager is asked to make a complex, multi-trait assessment of the employee's characteristics and abilities.

Finally, the form should contain room for whoever else must sign and make comments. There will be space for the employee's own signature, with an appropriate legend describing the degree of his involvement in the interview – he has attended the interview, or he agrees with the content of the document. Some firms leave a page for the employee to write his own comments on the form. The signature of the grandfather, or other manager with signing-off responsibility, is also recorded.

Though it would be wrong for us to suggest a standard appraisal form, because there is no standard appraisal system, we can be clear about the need to pilot whatever form is designed before releasing it. One becomes blind to the errors or misleading phrases in a form that has cost one hours of patient work; a friendly devil's advocate, who can cast a suspicious and a stupid eye over the form, is very necessary. Then give the form to one or two managers and ask them to fill it in, questioning them about the ease with which they understood the questions, the relative priorities given to each question, the amount of space provided, etc. It is odd, but common, to find that people make inferences about the importance of a question from the amount of space given it; and they will not often use a spare piece of paper if their thoughts overflow. So, part of the purpose in a pilot study is to give people an open space – more room on the form than they need – and then see what use they make of it.

Another reason behind the pilot study is to ease the task of processing the information from the appraisal system centrally. If, when completed forms come in, they are used to extract and record planning information of various kinds, then the clerical burden is reduced if the forms are designed for minimum backtracking and page-turning.

Preparation for appraisal forms

Mention has been made of the many uses to which preparation for appraisal, or preparation for counselling, forms can be put. Their role in encouraging participation in the interview and

motivation towards objectives achieved is difficult to over-
emphasise. In areas where individual objectives are difficult to
set because one's efforts depend upon other people – middle
management, continuous processing, matrix organisations, for
example – preparation for appraisal forms are invaluable; they
get the appraisee to do a job which the appraiser might find
impossible.

There are variations in the way these forms are used. One
important variation is whether the appraisee must bring the form
to the interview. If he must, then to a large extent the preparation
form duplicates the manager's appraisal form, though there need
not be complete overlap. This practice is useful wherever self-
assessment is required because the manager would have difficulty
appraising all the job or setting objectives for all the job. (This is
not as rare or as reprehensible as it might seem on the surface.
There are cogent reasons why self-appraisal leads to a fuller view
of the job.) On the other hand, there are firms where the preparation for counselling form is optional; it is sent to the employee as a
matter of course, but he pleases himself whether he fills it in, and
his manager may not ask to see it if he brings it to the interview.

A typical preparation for counselling form follows the same
basic logic as the manager's appraisal form – past, present,
future in particular, future in general. So, the form begins by
referring him back to last year's objectives; if he has them written
out then he refers to this list, if not he looks back to see what were
the chief activities he undertook. It is useful to follow this question with one in which the employee is asked to state a preference;
thus 'Which of your objectives satisfied you most? and least? and
why? or 'With which of your results are you most pleased? least
pleased? and why?' The objective behind this questioning is to
prompt the employee into examining his attiudes to the job and
the standards he sets himself.

Next follow questions about last year's performance as not
recorded in the objectives: did he experience any difficulties or
problems that had not been foreseen at the last appraisal? what
could he have done about them? what could his manager have
done about them? could anyone or anything else have helped
overcome them? Were there any special accomplishments last
year which were not foreseen during the last appraisal? Have
there been any special achievements outside the work context?

The next logical step is to ask questions about present performance. It is not usually wise to ask employees to give themselves a
specific performance rating; though most people will do this

sensibly, it is difficult to identify and deal with cases of abuse. This is why the questions we suggest for inclusion in a preparation for counselling form should get the employee thinking about the same things as his manager, but from a different angle. Present performance, for instance, can be approached with a question: Do you have any skills or abilities which your job does not presently use? Are there ways in which you, your manager, and the rest of the organisation could make your job more effective? Do you have any suggestions for making this a better place to work?

The future plans and aspirations are dealt with by questions such as: what sort of work would you like to be doing in five years' time? ten years' time? Are there parts of the firm about which you would like more information? What training or other experience do you think necessary to equip you to do your present job better? Can you foresee problems in the future that might interfere with good performance, and what help would you like in overcoming them?

Obviously, a form that contained all these questions would be overwhelming for the recipient; select and adapt as seems appropriate. It is even more important to leave lots of space for the employees thoughts on a preparation for counselling form; two questions per side of A4 paper is not unusual, and helps to give the impression that this is an important document and worth giving time to.

The provision of preparation for counselling, or preparation for appraisal, forms where none existed before is an intervention of some magnitude in the organisation's culture. Employee expectations will be raised, especially if the form is wide ranging; giving them a duplicate of the manager's appraisal form can be construed as enabling them to prepare their defence to a set of charges. An employee who has used such a form comes to the interview more prepared, readier to talk. It must be emphasised to managers that their role in such an interview is primarily to listen, to counsel, and to suggest, not to evaluate and lay down rules. To some managers this comes as a relief; to others it is a diminution of prerogative. Either way, it needs sensitive management and guidance from the manager of the appraisal system, and he should be alert to this need.

Finally in this chapter on system design, a note about the system's 'goodness of fit'. A system designed with specific purposes in mind, as in the chart of this chapter, stands a better chance of survival than an alien system or a Topsy. But no system is perfect, because a variety of purposes is served, compromises happen, people change, and the business changes. The reader who designs a new system will need to pilot every bit of it before going 'live', and should expect to have to make some changes after eighteen months or so. This is almost inevitable and does not mean that he was wrong to begin with. Like all good servo-mechanisms, the appraisal system needs at least two course corrections before staying on line. He will not get it right first time; but he will do a better job if he begins by seeking *simplicity* and a *reason for every feature* of the system.

Summary

The design of appraisal systems is governed by four groups of purposes: appraisee's, appraiser's, planning and control functions', and those imposed by external constraint. The mix of purposes selected has implications for who takes part in the appraisal; its degree of participativeness; the performance measures used; the type of target-setting involved; the ancillary information collected; grievance procedures; and who may see the appraisal forms. Appraisal form design follows on from system design; preparation for counselling forms increase the likelihood that the appraisee will participate thoughtfully in the appraisal interview.

5 Installing a system: training

Where the system has been designed and is ready to run, the managers who have to do appraisals need training. The reasons for this are many, and should not really require rehearsing for the committed reader; nonetheless managers are sometimes reluctant to be trained, so that persuasive arguments are needed. Some of these are:

(1) The appraisal interview is not like any other interview the manager is likely to have to conduct. It is private, usually, and the parties may be bound in confidence not to reveal what went on. It does not – should not – have the flavour of evaluation which selection interviews, and dismissal interviews, often have. It should also be participative (in most organisations), which distinguishes it from some other sorts of man-manager meetings.
(2) There is such a wide variety of purposes for which the appraisal system can be used, that it is important to get managers within one organisation using the system consistently and for that organisation's limited purposes. This is especially important if, for instance, managers believe that the system exists primarily to discipline them, or to set their salaries, and the designers of the system want to see it used for individual development purposes. When organisations grow by acquisition there are often some managers who have had different experience of appraisal from other managers.
(3) The appraisal system potentially places an important and useful tool in the hands of line managers. A skilful manager uses the appraisal system to get more from his employees, and more from himself, and increases morale at the same time. Nevertheless there are many appraisal systems which begin and end with paperwork issued by the personnel department. It is inevitable that the appraisal system starts with the personnel department, or with very senior managers; but if it is not to stay there, but pass into the hands of line managers who can use it, then those managers need training.

Training in appraisal is of two kinds. There is *knowledge* training, in which managers are taught the nuts and bolts of the system; and there is *skill* training, in which they learn to conduct

appraisal interviews well. In this chapter both types of training
are described, and procedures outlined for the reader to follow
when designing training. First, though, a warning about a third
purpose that sometimes creeps into appraisal training, usually
with disastrous results.

A training course, be it in knowledge or skills, is no place to get
managers' commitment to the principle of appraisal interviewing. Yet it often happens. In the worst case, the appraisal
system is designed by personnel experts with no consultation
with the line, and kept under wraps until it is revealed; senior
management give their commitment (though they probably
don't believe that appraisals will happen to *them*); middle
managers are not informed, and junior managers are put under
pressure to adopt the appraisal system for the wrong reason
(often for industrial relations reasons). In the midst of this confusion managers are gathered together in meetings to be told how
the system operates. At such meetings there are bound to be present some managers who will not learn how the system operates
until they feel they have been consulted about it. It only takes one
such manager to dig in his heels and the rest of the group cannot
progress in their learning. Such recalcitrance is easier to deal
with on a knowledge-giving course than on a skills-learning
course. But it could be avoided by simple precautions:

(a)   involve the line in setting the purposes of the appraisal
system, though not necessarily in the design of the system itself;
(b)   obtain commitment from the top and work downwards,
giving special attention to middle managers and to managers of
unusual functions;
(c)   start the cycle of appraisal interviews from the top and work
downwards, and make sure people know this is happening.

These measures lessen the risk of managers arriving for training while still wanting to argue the purpose of the appraisal
system.

Commitment meetings

Special efforts should be made to get managers' commitment to
the appraisal system before beginning training. It is difficult to
give general advice on a topic that is inevitably sensitive to
internal political issues; nonetheless, successful commitment

meetings usually meet some or all of the following conditions:

1 The person seeking commitment (afterwards referred to as the 'designer') has a clear statement of the suggested purposes the system is to achieve. He uses this statement to clarify any questions his audience might have which show they misunderstand the system's objectives; if any managers have previous experience of appraisal systems in this or other organisations then he makes sure that the purposes of this system are clarified and distinguished from previous practice.

2 The designer has with him examples of the proposed appraisal form, properly laid out and printed. He is willing to enter discussions about the purpose of the system (and indeed, if enough managers wish, he may want to alter the purposes of the system) but he is not prepared to negotiate about form design.

3 A tentative timetable for implementation of the system is ready for announcement.

4 An outside speaker of repute is there to give a homily on the advantages other firms have gained from the use of appraisal systems.

5 Syndicate work, if it is used at all, asks managers to examine *both* roles they will play in the appraisal system – appraiser and appraisee.

6 No deliberate attempt is made to describe the detailed operations of the appraisal system, or the skills required to interview, but if questions are asked about them then they are answered.

The reasons for these guidelines may need clarification. In particular, the first two may seem rigid. Our reason for suggesting that the designer should not negotiate on form design is only valid if the appraisal system has been designed to a given, agreed list of purposes. If this has happened, then the designer is saying to line managers: 'I am offering you a management tool. Currently it is set to achieve purposes X, Y, and Z. Using my professional skills I have designed the forms and the system to achieve those purposes. If you wish to substitute purposes A, B, and C, then I will advise on redesigning the system to achieve the new purposes; but I am not going to negotiate about how the present form and system design achieves purposes X, Y, and Z.' This is, of course, the position the good staff man can take up if he has the expertise. There are, however, many cases where the appraisal system has been designed without reference to an agreed set of purposes; where one firm has borrowed another firm's form, altering it here and putting in bits there, with no clear statement of objective. In this case the designer will not be able to settle arguments with line managers by referring them to the system's purposes, and he must cope like any other lost traveller without a map.

The use of an outside expert in commitment meetings is an example of the prophet being without honour in his own country. Often the outside expert is the appraisal designer for another firm, who is listened to with attention outside his own firm but has to call in his own outside expert when holding commitment meetings in-house. There is a large element of reassurance in the use of outside experts, letting managers know that they are not on their own. The outside expert needs, however, to be briefed to talk about the system of the firm he is visiting, and not about his own system.

Realistically, all one should expect from commitment meetings is an armed truce, or a watchful tolerance. Beware of trying to use them to whip up enthusiasm; for enthusiasm quickly dies away, and there is still hard work to be done. Clearing the ground of misconceptions; airing objections – which other managers often deal with more convincingly than the designer himself can; and demonstrating the designer's competence, is all that one should plan to achieve. Then the way is clear for training proper to begin.

Knowledge skills

This comes first in the training order. Unless people feel comfortable about filling in the forms and working the system, they will not be able to concentrate on the more subtle, and personal, appraisal skills. So it is important to separate the knowledge-giving part of the training from the skills part, maybe even having them on separate occasions.

A good beginning is to give the history of the appraisal system – why it was thought to be needed, who was involved in the design (stressing the line management involvement here, of course) and making reference, if appropriate, to the number of succesful companies who claim that appraisal systems help them manage better. Then move quickly on to the actual appraisal interview – the purpose of the interview, what happens in a typical interview, how the two parties feel about it, and so on. It is important to convey the feeling that appraisal is a personal tool of the manager concerned, to help him manage better. You can go into detail about the system for processing the appraisal information later; for the moment, concentrate on the fact that the interview is designed to help performance. Also, it helps to concentrate the minds of the listening managers if you remind them that not only will they be appraising, they will also be appraised.

At this stage the participants usually begin asking questions about the nuts and bolts of the system – how long an interview is likely to take, how frequently they will happen, etc. There will also be the inevitable comment 'That's what a good manager does anyway,' and we have given the trainer some possible replies to that statement in Chapter One. Be ready to tell them what training in appraisal skills will soon be forthcoming, if the discussion starts to veer that way.

The next logical step is to take them through the system which backs up the appraisal interviews. The details obviously depend upon the system you have designed, but do begin by disccussing the advantages – the collation of objectives, the putting together of training plans, the ability to do better manpower planning, the ability to monitor the performance of certain products or customers, the early detection and action on problem areas. A case study or two here does no harm, and your local Industry Training Board or the management journals often provide relevant material.

The point is, that even in this training module you are still to some extent 'selling' the system to the managers who use it, and if you can quote one or two instances of helpful appraisal systems you are using the old, but effective, salesman's trick of getting an endorsement from a famous personality.

It is notoriously difficult to put over information about new systems by lecturing to people; it is also a commonplace that managers tend not to read books and briefing material unless they are very short. So the trainer has a problem of getting the trainees to rehearse the new knowledge they have acquired in their short training session. One good way to do this is by making them use parts of the system.

1   Show them some appraisal forms that have been inadequately filled in. (Examples of faults: lack of detail in description of job performance, over-general description of next year's targets,

no comment and sign-off from the appraisee, training needs written as 'book him on a course', unsatisfactory performance recorded but no improvement plan noted.) You can illustrate these forms by projecting them onto a screen in front of the whole class, or you can give them to the trainees who solve the problem by working together in small groups. The latter takes longer but is probably more effective. The job they have to do is two-fold – to identify the faults, and then say what the consequences of those faults would be if they went uncorrected. An added refinement is to ask them whose responsibility it is to detect the faults. This exercise usually works very well in helping the trainees to put flesh on the bare bones of the system, and the trainer can add realism, in time, by selecting the 'howlers' from real appraisals. (Of course, if the training has been 100 per cent effective, there won't be any howlers, but such perfection is an unrealistic aim.)

2   Give them a small, self-scored questionnaire to fill in about the appraisal system. Such a questionnaire would ask about the frequency of appraisals, the coverage within the organisation, the aims of the system, the start-up date, the procedures for dealing with special cases, the procedures for dealing with delay, and so on. One refinement which the trainer can use later is to distribute a correct version of the questionnaire, bound in such a way that the managers can use it later as a reference document. Some large firms have gone to the expense of writing a programmed text to teach their managers how to use the appraisal systems; in a small firm the resources to do this may be lacking (though it could form a special project for someone suitable, like a trainee in personnel or a semi-redundant line manager). A simple questionnaire, thumb-indexed by topic, involves little extra labour after the training course itself has been designed.

The course in operating the appraisal system will probably be a short one. Half a day may suffice; it has been done in less time, and after the system is installed and running there may be no need to keep it as a separate training event – put it instead into the regular training programme for new managers. However, on the half-day training courses people will not ask all the questions they need answering, and so they should be supported by knowing a telephone number they can ring for any further information. It's surprising how often small points like this get neglected, thus adding to the line managers' feeling that they have been left holding personnel's baby.

Skills training

However good the forms, and however smooth the system, appraisal stands or falls by the quality of the appraisal interviews. Interviewing skills take second place in the calendar, after knowledge training, but this should not detract from their primacy. Indeed, appraisal interviewing skills are a well worn topic in the training literature, and there are many commercially available courses, of varying effectiveness.

Training in skills takes place only when two conditions are met. There must be *practice* in the skill, and there must be *knowledge of results* from practice, by which we mean that when one has done something well, one knows how well and the dimensions on which the goodness was measured. An appraisal skills programme differs greatly from a programme instructing about the workings of the system, in that on the skills programme the trainees spend a large amount of their time appraising. This they do by means of exercises. Their feedback, or knowledge of results, comes from the trainer, the other trainees, or some other measure. The exercises used to give people practice fall into three different kinds: role-play, real-life counselling, and live appraisal of real tasks.

Role-play

Typically, the trainer selects two people from the trainees and gives them 'roles' to learn. One role is that of the appraising manager, the other is that of the appraisee. The roles are selected so as to highlight particular managerial problems; for example, the appraisee may be performing poorly. Or he may have ambitions which his manager believes to be unrealistic. Or he and his manager may be in strong disagreement about the quality of his last year's work. Perhaps the appraisee thinks the manager has not done all he promised after the last appraisal, and is going to use this appraisal to challenge him. The range of possibilities is large. After spending a little time individually preparing themselves for the appraisal, the two trainees meet and conduct the interview with the rest of the trainees and the trainer looking on. After the interview the role-players are asked questions about their performance, and comments are invited from the observers.

Role-play is a seductively easy way of performing training. The trainer can use ready prepared role-descriptions, thus minimising the need for on-course adjustments to meet individual trainees' needs. The range of appraisal problems selected can cover a variety of topics thought to be representative of their training needs. However, role-play is not usually the best way of getting trainees to learn (if you measure learning by looking at changes in behaviour after the training course). The reason for this is that for most trainees, learning a new interpersonal skill is a fairly painful business. There is an implicit assumption that what one was doing before is somehow wrong. Many trainees on a skills training course pay lip-service to the notion of skill, but resist any attempt to change their own behaviour. It is therefore common to hear, after a role-play session where criticisms have been made of the way the role-play interview was conducted, comments such as 'Well, of course, it wouldn't have been like that in real life', or 'Of course, I only had half a sheet of paper to tell me the kind of guy I was supposed to be'. Comments like this tell the experienced trainer that the learning is somehow being held at arm's-length. On reflection some of the trainees may realise this, but the black-and-white, authoritarian manager who finds difficulty in putting himself into other people's shoes will not learn from such an experience – he will excel, by his very nature, in pushing the learning away from him.

The other course members often find difficulty in following a role-play. It's not surprising. The trainer is effectively saying to them 'Fred is pretending to be Joe, and he is appraising Jack who is pretending to be Dennis. The rest of you pay attention and learn something.' The conceptual twists in the spiral are difficult enough, and they are not there to learn conceptual inputs, but to change their own behaviour. It is small wonder that many of the audience's comments after a role-play appraisal interview are phrased as 'I thought you played him very well', or 'It was quite a realistic performance', indicating the difficulty they are having in separating the wood from the trees.

A good trainer will try to overcome these difficulties by briefing the audience thoroughly before the role-play actually starts, and by giving them a structure to help them in their task of observing – they will be asked to look at who does most of the talking, or to assess the balance between past, present and future. However, we have little doubt that most of the audience are still confused by the part-acting, part real-life nature of the role-play, and as their own part is essentially passive they have not much incentive to try to overcome the difficulties.

There is another problem associated with role-play appraisals;

only two people can take part at a time, and the rest are inactive. This means that on (say) a two-day course with twelve participants, each trainee may be actively involved once or at the most twice; the rest of the time he is watching other people. As one of the essences of skill-learning is the opportunity to practise, it is obvious that a role-play course fails to meet this criterion for most of the time.

Another objection to role-play is the way it is often used. Role-play exercises come automatically to too many trainers who cannot in all honesty be bothered to think of anything else. On in-house and on public courses we have seen role-plays used which were taken from another industry, another country, or another decade. Some of the trainees reacted with contempt, others with puzzlement; very few of them learned anything, and that happened by accident, not by the trainer's planning. A sensitively planned training course involves all the trainees; offers them practice in new skills at a pace neither too easy nor too difficult; does not give them the chance to hold the learning at arm's length; and does not manipulate the dynamics of the group so that people resolve the frustration they felt by finally praising the course. Most courses using role-play exercises do not meet these criteria; this is not inherent in the nature of role-play, but poor trainers have done role-play a disservice by misuse of the technique.

A skilled trainer can use an ordinary role-play interview and, by confrontation and gentle questioning, prevent people running away from the learning implicit therein. He will not let the participants escape by claiming that the interview was not 'real life', and he will extract structured observations from the onlookers. However, there are two especial learning purposes which role-play can serve, and the skilled trainer will use these. They are:

1 *Putting yourself in the other's shoes.* Experiments with attitude change clearly show that one good way of effecting such a change is to get the trainee to take the part of someone whose attitude is different from his. For example, if you want trainees to understand what it's like to feel underprivileged, get them to act the part of a woman or a black who feels passed over for promotion. A manager who will have to appraise, in the next year or two, a lot of people anxious for career growth in a static environment, will do a better job if on a training programme he has had to role-play one or more such people. This will do far

more for his performance as a manager than being asked to role-play an appraising manager turning down such people's requests, although if it is possible to have him play both roles then that opportunity should be taken. Whatever the company policy which the appraisals are administering, the appraising manager will do a better job if he understands the feelings of those being appraised. A skilled trainer will select role-plays – probably writing them himself to ensure greater authenticity – in which appraising managers can get a better feeling for the points of view of those they must appraise.

2   *Trying on a new appraisal personality*. A training course should be a place to experiment with new ways of doing things, in the knowledge that the consequences don't matter. Occasionally the trainer finds that his trainees are unwilling to unbend, reluctant to try new ideas. This often happens in firms where appraisal systems, or other management devices, have gone wrong or been installed with little support; in order to survive, managers have learned a routine which they feel safe with, and they are not going to break that routine for a training course. Here the trainer may select role-plays that demand new behaviours from the trainees. He may offer a role-play and ask the appraiser to make all the mistakes he can think of; or to act as if he were himself the victim of a poor appraisal; or to act as he believes a well known television personality would perform the appraisal. By this request the trainer is forcibly shaking one or both parties out of their old habits, while making it 'safe' to do so by the offer of an alias. Such a manoeuvre opens up the possibility of later experiments without the need for a shield.

Real-life counselling

In the second common appraisal exercise, the artificiality of role-play is abandoned. Interviews still take place in front of observers, but the appraiser and appraisee discuss a real-life problem brought to the interview by the appraisee. It is likely that on most training courses the appraiser and appraisee will not be in a direct reporting relationship to each other. Sometimes the appraisal interview covers the last year's performance as well as the present problem and the future; more often, though, this exercise is used to develop counselling skills and the requirement to appraise past performance in detail is waived.

There is no doubt that trainees find this situation realistic. The observers often have to be restrained, in their reporting-back, from putting themselves into the appraising manager's shoes with a 'Well, if I were you, I'd have told him to do so-and-so', and the trainer must expect difficulty in keeping everyone's attention concentrated on the *way* the problem was solved rather than the solution actually achieved.

Appraising managers learn from the very newness of the situation, if the trainer so structures things. Often the appraising manager will ask how he is expected to counsel someone with a problem that he was not expecting – 'If this were back at work I'd have had an inkling that this would come up at the appraisal', he will say. For the trainer this is the chance to discuss the importance of *listening* in the counselling interview, as the manager – who may be a complete stranger to the problem – learns some of the keywords by which he can get the appraisee outlining the problem and himself discovering his own solution. Indeed, here lies the prime strength of this exercise: it enables the trainer to concentrate on counselling skills and skills of joint problem-solving. In the early stages of training by using real-life counselling tasks, some of the commonest managerial mistakes can be guaranteed to occur; for example, an appraisee offered, as his problem for counselling, the fact that he desperately wished to give up smoking and would welcome the opportunity to talk about it. The appraising manager responded immediately with, 'Well, it's a filthy habit, I'm sure you know that, and it ruins your health and the comfort of the people around you and I won't have it in my office for a start . . .', thus committing a number of the cardinal sins of counselling. The observers, who were equipped with a list of sins to look for, were convulsed with laughter; until it came to the turn of some of them, and they realised just how easy it was to step into the trap and how a real effort of will was needed by the appraising manager to make himself listen.

Counselling training using real-life problems demands rather more of the trainer, and it presents potential political difficulties because the problems are real. It also has a danger, opposite to that of role-play, of being too near to real life for the trainees to concentrate on *how* counselling is done rather than on *what* is achieved. However, the benefits outweigh the disadvantages and this is the method we would recommend for training in counselling.

Live appraisal of real tasks

Here we present a module for basic appraisal training which we developed ourselves in response to a good deal of dissatisfaction with role-play appraisals. The aim is to involve all the trainees in appraising real people doing real tasks. There is an underlying pattern to the exercise, which can then be varied at will:

(a) a volunteer does something appraisable, before the other trainees;

(b) everybody except the volunteer prepares to appraise the performance while the volunteer prepares to be appraised;

(c) the trainer selects one person to do the appraisal;

(d) the appraiser appraises the volunteer, while the rest of the trainees observe;

(e) all the rest prepare to appraise the appraisal; the appraiser prepares to be appraised; the original performer can rest;

(f) the trainer selects one person to appraise the appraiser;

(g) the first appraiser is himself given an appraisal interview while the rest observe;

(h) together they review the exercise.

Some of the advantages of this module are obvious. There is little slack time for anyone; they all have to prepare to appraise, even if they are not called on to perform an appraisal. And there is, written into the actual exercise, the opportunity to appraise an appraisal interview formally, instead of having the group watch an interview and then make comments.

The first stage of the module – volunteer's party piece – takes ten to fifteen minutes. In a course of two or three days, the module is run a number of times, and in the early stages the volunteer's task is likely to be simple and unimportant, like giving a short talk, or drawing a diagram. As the course progresses, 'party pieces' can be more directly relevant to the work content.

Stage (b) takes fifteen to twenty minutes, and the appraisal (Stage (c)), is fifteen minutes long. Stage (d) similarly takes fifteen to twenty minutes, followed by a fifteen-minute appraisal, and the group review can take up to half an hour. Four or five of these modules can be fitted into a day's training, therefore, and the content of the modules varied to address different training needs.

For example, it is possible to alter the module so as to concentrate on *appraisal for improvement.* Here the volunteer repeats his party piece after the first appraisal, and is appraised a second time before the appraising manager is himself appraised. This usually provokes a good deal of thought about the need to be specific in setting goals and objectives. With a little manipulation from the trainer the hoary problem of measurement of performance by subjective judgement can be examined, if the party piece is one on which different people could take different views of its quality.

Another alteration we have found valuable is to use the pressures on the first-line manager as the topic for appraisal. Here we take a group of six to eight trainees. One is appointed the boss, and one is the team leader; the rest are slaves. The team leader's task is, together with his slaves, to build a tower from Lego bricks according to design standards which the boss has set. Early in the proceedings, then, the boss is given the bricks and the necessary information, and in his free time he must arrive at a design. He can please himself whether he involves the team leader. At their first formal meeting, under the eyes of the rest of the trainees, boss and team leader plan their activities; boss then withdraws as the team leader and slaves build. Boss then appraises team leader on his performance as a manager of the team of slaves; sometimes there will be a second building, so that the boss is also appraising for improvement. The pressures on the first-line manager – loyalties to boss and to subordinates, difficulties of working with unclear instructions or to a standard he doesn't approve of, being held responsible for what is, in effect, someone else's performance – all these are thrown into high relief by this exercise. We find the boss team leader/slaves variant invaluable; from time to time this exercise leads to important insights. Once, the boss set for the team leader a design which he had not consulted the leader about, and which was impractical under the circumstances; the team leader tried to build, but the tower fell down; at appraisal time the atmosphere became so heated that the team leader resigned, and said he was taking the slaves with him. Boss and team leader together went to see the slaves, to explain what had happened. In the ensuing discussion, as loyalties formed and re-formed, shop stewards emerged, conservatives and radicals fought over principles and all learned a great deal about industrial relations and the job the first-line manager faces.

This module seems to have a number of advantages over the

role-play model, and we have been able to compare the two. In one large firm approximately half the managers were trained by a traditional, well liked role-play appraisal course, while the other half were trained on a course made up of variants on the modules given above. Both courses lasted the same length of time, and were given by trainers of comparable standing in the eyes of the organisation; as far as we could tell, there was no systematic difference between the trainees who went on the role-play course and those who went on the modular course. At the end of the courses themselves, the trainee's reactions did not differ according to which course they were on; there was a slight but non-significant bias in favour of the role-play course. Eighteen months later, though, the modular-trained managers were very nearly up-to-date as far as overdue appraisals were concerned, while the role-play ones had an average backlog of nine months; and reference to attitude survey data showed that when the subordinates were asked about their satisfaction with their last appraisal interview, the subordinates of the modular-trained managers were, on average, one point more satisfied on a five-point scale.

In summary, then, for appraisal skills training a combination of live appraisal of real tasks, and real-life counselling exercises, is most likely to produce results, as measured by changes in behaviour after the training course.

Feedback

We mentioned at the beginning of this chapter that training in a new skill involves both practice and feedback. The exercises outlined above are the vehicles for practice; what about the feedback on performance? where is that to come from?

Training courses in appraisal offer the trainees three sources of knowledge of results: the other trainees, the trainer, and himself. Most training courses pause after each exercise while the observing trainees make comments upon the performers – be they role-players, counsellor and counselled, or volunteer and appraiser. The trainer may or may not join in these comments. Whether or not they are helpful to the performers depends upon a number of factors:

(a) comments should be *balanced*; good performance and bad performance should both be remarked upon;

(b) comments should be *detailed*; general statements are of less help than comments on particular interchanges;

(c) comments should be *objective*; they should say what the commentator saw, not how he evaluated it;

(d) comments should be *about what actually happened*, not about what the commentator thinks should have happened, or would have done himself.

If these conditions are not met, then the performers will not know the specific aspects of their performance that made it successful or unsuccessful. Without this knowledge they will be unable to make systematic improvements to their performance, nor will they learn how to monitor their own performance. Yet the average observer – say a trainee on an appraisal course ordered to watch a role-play or counselling interview – does not observe to these standards. Asked to comment on the performance of the participants in the interview, he will say things like: 'I think you did it very well, you put him at his ease and made him feel comfortable, and I think you listened well . . .' or 'I don't like the way you kept cutting him off whenever he tried to tell you something. I kept noticing that whenever he wanted to say something you wouldn't let him finish . . .' or 'If I'd been you I wouldn't have let him get away with that excuse about production not having the stuff ready on time'. The first of these comments is too general to be of any use to a trainee who wants to know what he did right so he can do it again. The second is detailed enough, but is confined exclusively to things he did wrong. And the third comment reduces, in semantic content, to the phrase beloved of arm chair performers everywhere: 'If I were you I'd have done it about right'. This is why it is important to give the people who are watching an appraisal interview a structure against which to make their observations and to arrange their feedback. In time, as observers become participants and revert back to being observers, they will incorporate the structure so that they learn to monitor they own performance.

Observers should be asked to look for concrete phenomena, such as:

who opened the conversation, appraiser or appraisee?
did the appraiser begin by asking, 'How do you think you did?'
what was the balance of talking between appraiser and appraisee?

who interrupted whom? what with? how often?
what questions did the appraiser ask to broaden the issue?
what questions did the appraiser ask to narrow it down?
how often did the appraiser flatly contradict the appraisee?
how often did the appraiser support, or build on, the
appraisee's own ideas?
how did the appraiser use and control silence in the interview?
how did the appraiser cope when he didn't know the answer?
how were standards of performance evolved?
how was the interview concluded?

The list above, which is by no means exhaustive, progresses from
the specific to the general. We suggest that observers begin by
confining their attentions to matters so concrete they can be
counted, and progress later to monitoring the more sophisticated
questions when they have become used to the skills involved in
being an impartial observer. Then, as the training progresses,
with the help of the trainer, trainees will learn to monitor their
own performance – again beginning with the simple things and
going on to learn more complex skills

The training options

The reader will have noted that we do not outline in this chapter a
standard training course. Indeed, we have been deliberately
vague about the content of some of the exercises and some of the
items in the observers' check-lists. This is because we believe that
packaged training programmes in this area may do more harm
than good. Each appraisal system is unique, and the managers
operating it are unique. Better to spend a little effort designing
something custom-tailored, within the guidelines offered here,
than to put in a programme wholesale and wait for it to cause
problems, as it surely will. Better always to design appraisal
exercises using your own firm's problems than to borrow from
another industry or organisation. Better to get people on courses
discussing their own appraisal skills and their own needs, rather
than keeping the learning distant by using role-plays. It takes a
little more work, but is well worth it in terms of the later learning.
  Appraisal training must take its place in the training priorities
with all other sorts of training. We are sometimes asked how long

should be devoted to it, whether it will mix with other topics, etc. Training in the workings of the appraisal system needs from two hours to half a day, depending upon the sophistication and experience of the managers; if they have already been appraised themselves, for instance, then the training time can be shorter. Training in appraisal skills is a longer job, and with the average untrained manager we advocate a two-day training course as the minimum. The appraisal system training mixes well with other inputs about the management information system, and could form part of a training course on this topic. Appraisal skills training, on the other hand, mixes better with subjects like grievance handling, counselling and coaching skills, negotiation training, industrial relations training, and so on. We have sometimes seen appraisal interviewing mixed with selection interviewing; they are not bedfellows whom we would encourage to lie together.

With commercially available courses it is important to distinguish training in skills from training in the system. Some courses attempt to do both, and fail to meet either objective. There are good commercial courses which serve as an introduction to the whole topic of appraisal, and would be useful to the system designer or personnel manager. Then there are mixed courses, in which system design is mixed with role-play appraisal interviews; these are likely to be successful only if entry is strictly monitored. Otherwise the mix of personnel directors who want to know about appraisal systems, and line managers who have been sent to improve their personal skills, will not 'take'. We have seen very few commercial courses which successfully tackle the problem of increasing appraisal skills, and if your own organisation is too small to support an in-house training course for managers then our recommendation is to discuss the matter with your Industry Training Board, to see if their specialists can tailor a course to meet your needs along with some similar firms.

Finally, there is a training option taken up by one firm which deserves mention for its resourceful approach to a problem that sometimes occurs when the appraisal system has been installed for some time – managerial apathy. Personnel department grumbled that no incentive, warning, or threat, was strong enough to make managers do appraisals unless they absolutely had to; and then the interviews were skimped and the paperwork unhelpful. A trainer designed, and ran, a series of training courses that trained *appraisees* how to be appraised. Of course, the response was tremendous, as people below managerial level saw this as offering them at least an equal part in the management of performance appraisal. In sheer self-defence, managers began asking for courses in how to appraise. They were told that the training department was fully committed to courses on being appraised, but that the managers were welcome to attend these courses themselves. A number of managers did so, to find an unlooked-for learning bonus; for, just as taking a course of instruction for buyers makes one a better salesman, so taking a course on how to be appraised did wonders for the performance of these laggardly managers. The trainer can learn from these tactics, not merely for arousing interest in his courses; for another lesson, often forgotten, is that in mock appraisals on training courses the appraisee is not just there to enable people to have an appraisal to watch; he himself has the opportunity to learn a great deal about appraisals by being on the receiving end of one of them.

Summary

Appraisal training has two main purposes: increasing knowledge, and increasing skills. Neither purpose can be served if the trainees are not committed to the appraisal system; so commitment meetings must come first. Skills training is helped by practical exercises of three kinds: role-play, real-life counselling, and live appraisal of real tasks. The latter two give the skilled trainer more flexibility in meeting the real training needs of managers on the course, and role-play is not as useful, except for certain limited purposes, as the other methods.

6 Monitoring and control

So far the patient reader has been taken through the design of an appraisal system from the earliest stages – thoughts about the organisation's purposes and how the system helps achieve them – through to getting managers trained and ready to operate the system. He would be forgiven for thinking that his work is now at an end and that all he has to do is wait for the information to come in and the people perform better. Alas, it is not so. The appraisal system can go seriously wrong in the first eighteen months of its existence unless it is closely monitored, and it will always require a watchful eye. At times of change or crisis – reorganisation, expansion, contraction, pay restraint, for example – the appraisal system is vulnerable and could become distorted or fall into disuse.

This chapter describes ways in which the appraisal system can be monitored by its designer or a personnel specialist. We begin by warning that some of the changes that inevitably take place in the system's first few months will be good ones and should not be resisted. Unless line managers feel that the system belongs to them, they will not use it with commitment; and in making it belong they may alter it to fit. Before personnel worries them into restoring the original form, it is worth asking whether the change is, in fact, an improvement. Consider the firm where managers were instructed to conduct appraisal interviews in their office, with the usual injunctions to observe privacy, peace and quiet. They discovered later that many managers were completing the first part of the interview in the office, but adjourning to the local pub for a more free-ranging discussion about careers, training needs, and next year's mission. The personnel department were on the point of issuing strict instructions that this must stop when it was pointed out to them that many interview participants valued the informality and change of scene; it helped them get away from day-to-day pressures and take the long view for once. Personnel department duly confined themselves to reminding people that on no account should appraisal interview documents be taken out of the company buildings, and no great harm appears to have befallen them.

Some common system failings

In the early days of an appraisal system it is surprising how much
sheer *misunderstanding of terms* exists amongst the people
involved. It is not enough to define concepts once, or even three
times; definitions and uses must be hammered home. As
indicated earlier, the word *objective* is frequently given varying
meanings by different people; *aim, target, goal,* or similar
synonyms are also vulnerable. The most dangerous misunder-
standings centre on whether it should in fact be attainable, and
whether it should be numerically measurable. Misunderstanding
is reduced by getting managers to exchange definitions of the
term – training courses and visits to managers' meetings are suitable occasions – and perhaps by publishing for managers a sample of the kinds of objectives you would like to have set. And the
reader should not get bothered by the semantic jungle himself – as long as there is consistent practice and he is aware of the
need to check others' understanding.

Other common words which are misunderstood are *training,
training need,* and *development.* There are organisations where
training is seen as a way of remedying deficiencies; talk of training needs is, by definition, implying a specific deficiency in performance, and may be seen as a condemnation. *Diagnosis of training needs* is not a good phrase to use to an engineer, as most
engineers equate diagnosis with fault-finding. An appraisal
system borrowed from another firm may contain words which
have emotional overtones in one's own firm; people recruited
from another firm may find meanings which were not intended.
There are organisations where no distinction is made between
the terms *training* and *development*; others where training refers
to improvements in the performance of the present job and
development is improvement for the next job; there are others
where training is applied to the job-holder and development is
applied to the job. The reader who is not alert for such possible
nuances may find himself getting to confused arguments when
talking about the appraisal system.

Then there are words which the personnel department uses
one way, and line managers another. *Personality,* as used by
psychologists and personnel specialists, is a neutral term describing the kind of character, attitudes, and style someone has; to
other people *personality* is something you have a lot of if you're
Shirley Bassey or President Carter. *Performance, behaviour,*

and *attitude*, all carry a strong flavour of evaluation for some people. And there are phrases, like *let's have a look at your strengths and weaknesses*, which personnel people often take for granted but which may strike terror into the heart of an appraisee who has never heard them before. This is why it is important to involve line managers in planning and implementing the system, and to get documents and instructions read over by people unfamiliar with appraisals and personnel systems; and then check at regular intervals by asking people what terms like *objective* mean to them.

As well as misunderstanding the terms, people can *misunderstand the system*. This may show itself in forms sent to the wrong place, or given wider circulation than they should, or appraisals being done selectively. To some extent this can be checked centrally if simple data are collected from each appraisal form as they come in. Look for patterns: are there managers who are consistently late, give consistently high, or low, ratings, who write little on the form? Are there particular kinds of employee who figure high, or low, in completed appraisals? Are they concentrating on poor performers, high flyers, leaving out those above age fifty? An afternoon spent studying appraisal returns with a pocket calculator often reveals interesting facts; calculating the probability that a manager whose own appraisal is overdue will keep his own people waiting, for example.

There was once a multinational organisation where it was discovered that all the performance ratings, for everyone in one small country, were grade C or below. On investigation, the cause of the trouble was found to be the country general manager, who said: 'I myself am rated only a C performer. If I am a C, then it stands to reason that no one working for me can be better than a C.' Though this was presented as a logical point, the psychological aspects of his decision did not go unnoticed.

In another multinational, where performance appraisal ratings were used for salary planning purposes and where a slowdown in growth had resulted in more people receiving high ratings (they stayed in their jobs longer), another interesting misunderstanding occurred. Salary planning was done in the expectation of a normal distribution of performance ratings. When more people were rated towards the top of the scale, the salary planning department raised the alarm. Somewhat unthinkingly, a senior manager sent out instructions to all managers in all the countries affected, telling them that in future the perfor-

mance appraisal ratings within their department must conform
to a normal curve. Most managers reacted to this by filing the
communication in their wastebaskets; some, in research and
development or other special departments, replied that no one
worked in these departments who was not a star performer. One
country, Germany, took the message seriously and at the end of
the year each department returned a normal distribution of performance ratings; in some cases this had involved managers in
bribing other managers to transfer to them their poor performers, a move that was normally forbidden. Quota was made
up, but the appraisal system suffered somewhat.

The people best motivated to make sense of the appraisal
system are the people who will themselves be appraised. It is
good strategy to address them when trying to get the system
understood. Employees on joining should be told about the
appraisal system – not just on their first day, when they are bewildered by all the other things that happen to them, but as an
integral part of their induction into the firm. Some firms go as far
as setting 'induction objectives' with the new employee; this
enables better induction to take place and also alerts the
employee to the appraisal interview which he can expect six
months or so after joining. The employee may then press his
manager for the appraisal interview, so reducing the chance that
the manager will put it off. Someone should be available to answer employees' queries – either direct or through their union representative – on the same terms as managers have their queries
answered.

Of course, all managers are appraised and do appraisals; yet it
is in their role as appraisee that they are more permeable to
information about how the appraisal system works. This is why
training *to be appraised* is such a success, in terms both of
attitude change and skill improvement.

In the early days of an appraisal system a pattern can be set
which it will be difficult to change later. Typically this includes
commitment in principle from the top, poor briefing to middle
managers, and pressure exerted on first-line managers to complete their appraisals whatever else may be happening. This pressure comes from a number of sources: because publicity will have
gone out to employees, so they will expect it from him; because
poor performance is often easier to identify at this level and the
appraisal scheme is seen as a way of managing it; because
objectives for middle managers are difficult to formulate, but not

so for non-managers, and so on. Great care should be exercised to prevent this happening, as it is difficult to root out once established; people lose faith in the motivational aspects of the appraisal system and it becomes a paper-chase. Prevention is, however, not easy. A rule that events must start from the top and work down is useful; e.g that no one may do an appraisal until he himself has been appraised. Training should start at the top, even if this means sending directors on expensive external courses or having them visited by prestige outsiders. Middle managers too should be thoroughly briefed and trained. This may entail going outside the immediate field of appraisal systems for a while, to discuss the manager's job in general. This is because the middle manager's job involves co-ordinating the work of other managers; so, he has to set *managerial* objectives for his people, be able to detect *management* problems, and have clear and communicable insights into the business of *managing*. Not many middle managers do this well; they see themselves as grown-up first-line managers, or senior specialists, or directors-in-waiting. Many of them have difficulty in setting objectives for managers because they lack a robust vocabulary with which to discuss management.

From time to time managers experience difficulty appraising the work of their subordinates when the subordinates exercise a special skill which the manager does not share. Here the problem is likely to be one of attitude – the subordinate feeling that the manager is not competent to judge, perhaps, or the manager feeling diffident or even jealous. These problems also occur when the manager is in a different location from the subordinate. Again, this is a problem more easily prevented than cured. The subordinate should receive a preparation for counselling form, or perhaps his own copy of the performance appraisal form, on which he can appraise his own performance. Margerison[1] argues powerfully for the use of self-appraisal schemes and stresses their benefits in situations where the manager might not know everything about the job to be done. Consideration should also be given to the use of two appraisers, one for technical matters only, and the manager doing the rest. One firm uses the 'uncle' system – someone on a level with the appraising manager, and known to both parties, can be called upon for advice, assistance, or second opinions should either party request it. Yet another course of action, for firms where a number of people work independently of their managers for most of the time, is the appraisal system organised by Money Brothers and described in Chapter Two.

These kinds of problem, where people feel incompetent to take part in the appraisal process, can only be discovered by going into the organisation and asking people how they felt about their recent experiences with appraisal. Later in this chapter we quote from two attitude surveys on appraisal schemes which the reader may want to borrow to monitor his system; but in the early days of appraisals there is no substitute for intelligent listening to the people who have had to conduct them. Now it is an odd fact of life that many personnel executives are worst treated of all in respect of personnel policies. One of us once had the job of exhorting busy line managers to do more and better appraisal interviews, while painfully conscious of not having had an interview for over two years, and this is by no means an uncommon experience. This is a case for imposing yet another rule – that line managers should not be chivvied about appraisals while there are any outstanding in the personnel department.

Other problems emerging in the early stages of the schemes may derive from appraisers being unsure of the terms in which they are required to answer. A common example, referred to earlier, concerns questions about training and development needs. Some people find it impossible to think of training needs without expressing them as training courses, so that the question: 'What training does he require to equip him to do his present job better?' elicits the answer: 'Communications course, computer familiarisation course, and leadership course'. In practice managers use courses in a number of ways; for training, for reward, for punishment, for a short holiday and as a way of giving status. It is better if they can be encouraged to state the particular skill or knowledge area which needs improving; they can recommend a course also, but only after having thought about the performance areas which the course is intended to improve. Similar considerations apply to questions like: 'What kind of post do you see him occupying in five years' time?'

Research into existing systems

An appraisal system that has been established for some time will need checking. After a few years people become blasé. Managers query the value of appraising people who have been in their jobs a long time and are likely to continue that way. Local variations in the use of performance ratings go beyond the tolerance of the personnel department. Managers discover that the world does not collapse immediately if they forget to do appraisals. More importantly, organisations change direction – products change, markets change, suppliers change, people change. What was appropriate ten years ago, by way of interview style and performance ratings, may not be appropriate today. The department with responsibility for the appraisal system should, from time to time, do a little research. Four examples of research strategies are given below.

Checking appraisal action

The researcher takes a sample of appraisal forms and notes the suggestions for future actions that were made, e.g. commitments made for training during the following year. Then he checks to see whether these actions were carried out, in this example by going to the training records to discover if training was in fact implemented, and when. If the records exist this is not a difficult exercise, and leads to useful results; Ed Moorby, of the Air Transport and Travel Industry Training Board, quotes a case of a firm where one stood twice as much chance of going on a training course if training had *not* been recommended during the appraisal than if it had. Such simple information, starkly presented, began a thorough discussion of why that firm's employees were disillusioned with the appraisal system. Commitments to special assignments or projects can also be followed through in this way. A more time-consuming piece of research, but worth while when there are serious problems, is to follow from top to bottom a slice of the organisation, looking at the kinds of objectives that are set, the amount of detail gone into on the appraisal records, the presence or absence of appraisee comments and their contents. This progress chart may illustrate bottlenecks, places where the appraisal system changes purpose, places where the objectives at the top are lost sight of, and so on. Simple content analysis of the type of objective set, and the type of performance standards, tells one a great deal. As Management by Objectives systems depend upon all the links in the chain being strong, the identification of weak links is the first stage in the process of changing the MbO system, or the organisation, or both.

One small firm used analysis of the appraisal records to check the success of its training programme. The fullness, attention to detail, and objectivity of the appraisal forms were rated on a three-point scale, and bar charts drawn for each question. The first sample was taken from a group of untrained managers, and this was compared visually with charts drawn for samples of trained managers. There was a healthy move towards fullness and thoughtfulness and away from subjectivity as more managers received training. The charts gave a quick, graphic picture of the way appraisal forms were being filled in, and thereby allowed inferences about the way interviews were being conducted; they also were of use in training programmes and in the commitment-getting meetings which proved necessary as the firm grew by acquisition.

All in-house research suffers from difficulties caused by the fact that the researchers live in the place they are researching. Research should start with an open mind, and with a hypothesis for the research to test. Doing in-house research makes it difficult to have an open mind – one knows the people, and one would not begin the research if one did not suspect the possible problem. One must be doubly careful to avoid research that merely confirms one's prejudices; so, if the reader decides to check the appraisal actions, his precautions should include: taking a random sample of records, not including any because they look interesting or discarding any because they are known to be exceptional; getting at least one other person to check his analysis independently, without knowing the researcher's results; and if he interviews other people in the course of his research, he must avoid suggesting to them the answer he would like or expect them to give.

Checking appraisal predictions

In 1976 the Institute of Manpower Studies, through their Co-operative Research Programme, conducted a survey of the methods firms use to assess managerial potential. The large majority of those studied assessed potential by means of the manager recording on the performance appraisal form his opinion of the man's potential. When they were asked what methods they used to validate this system some of them required the concept of validation to be spelt out more fully, and to most of them it had never occurred to check to see if the predictions of potential had been borne out in practice. Yet, work elsewhere (reported in Stewart and Stewart[2]) has shown that enormous improvements can be made to business performance by checking the validity of the assessment methods.

Any predictions made in an appraisal interview can be, and should be, checked. If managers are asked to rate someone's potential, in terms of how far advanced he will be in a given number of years, then it is possible to check how many of these predictions are correct. It is also possible, and more important, to check how many people predicted as having potential for certain levels of management are *performing well* in those jobs. Simple statistics to iron out the effects of seniority, business growth, etc., then enable one to place a measure on the truth of the manager's prediction.

A simpler way of checking the same problem is available in firms where a list of high potential people is kept; one checks to see whether position on the list is in any way related to subsequent promotion. Many firms who have over-computerised their personnel systems have such lists. The man at the top may have been there for two years as appointing managers select from under him! Or in many cases the appointing managers write man-specifications that place heavy emphasis on 'local knowledge'. With assessments of potential, or other measures that affect career growth, the necessity to validate one's system grows apace as employment legislation brings managers' decision-taking mechanisms under scrutiny.

Predictions given in the rest of the organisation can also be checked against appraisal data. One common example is the checking of the selection method. We once correlated the performance on an aptitude test with performance at initial training school, and performance on both these measures with performance in the first year in the field; the surprising result was that performance on the test correlated very highly with performance in training school, but that there was a negative correlation between both these measures and performance out in the field. This simple check enabled much better use to be made of the aptitude test, and some useful re-organisation of the training. Again, we stress our belief that selection methods will become exposed to the same scrutiny in the UK as they have in the US, with the consequent need to show validation data for psychological tests and other selection instruments; the performance appraisal system is potentially a very useful source of both validation data and ideas for improving the selection system.

Another example of the use of appraisal data for research is the talent drain index. To calculate this, draw a graph showing numbers of people against performance rating – which will probably look like a normal distribution that has skewed towards the top of the scale. Use only the appraisal records for the last six months or year. Then draw the same graph showing the performance ratings of those people who left during the same period of time. This is a useful piece of information for any discussion about manpower strategy – if top performers are over-represented in the leavers, then remedial action may be needed. The index is quickly calculated, and provides a way of introducing performance appraisal data into the more qualitative and subtle areas of management decision-making – too often the appraisal scheme is seen as having implications only for people in salary planning departments.

Surveying employee attitudes

Asking the employees what they think of the appraisal system is usually a sound idea, and many firms have done so, either by a separate survey or through the regular processes of checking employee attitudes to all aspects of their jobs. Williams[3] quotes one attitude survey in which respondents were asked the following questions:

> Do you have a clear idea of what specific end results are expected in your job?
> To what extent are there adequate opportunities for discussing the scope, end results, problems, and constraints of your job with your superiors?
> Do you have a clear idea of what your superior thinks about (a) your current performance, (b) your potential and future prospects?
> To what extent do you and he discuss those areas where you need to improve results?
> To what extent are you and your superior frank about personal factors which either enhance or restrict your effectiveness, e.g. your relationship with him, the support you give each other, your relationships with others, your

capacity to see jobs through, your managerial skills generally, etc.?
To what extent do discussions about personal and behavioural factors provide you and your chief with a basis for improving work relationships and your joint effectiveness?

Williams used this questionnaire to survey a number of companies. He found that in general there was satisfaction with the way job problems were handled, less satisfaction about the way personal factors were handled, and a good deal of ignorance about the superiors' views on potential and future prospects.

In Appendix 6.1 at the end of this chapter we quote an attitude survey developed in-house by one firm anxious to get its employees' feelings about the appraisal system and other career development data. People are asked how they feel about the frequency of appraisals, the length of time they take, the actions that are taken as a result of the interview, and the use of talent in general. This is a good example of such an in-house survey. It is well laid out, the questions are simple but not simplistic, there is a good coverage of the main and related topics, and plenty of room for people to give additional information.

However, no attitude survey is of any use unless it is actually *managed* afterwards. For employees to participate wholeheartedly they must feel that the information they give will be made use of, not just filed away somewhere. Attitude surveys normally generate two separate kinds of data: locally useful data, and organisational data. For instance, Question 21 in Appendix 6.1. asks for employees' views on the openness and constructiveness of the appraisal interview as they see it. This is information which individual managers need, to do their managerial jobs with, and defects cannot really be remedied by action from the centre; far better to give individual managers information on the opinions of the people who report to them – rendered anonymous, of course – so that they can take action themselves. At the other extreme, the answers to Question 28, in which employees are asked whether they feel that useful talent has been passed over during the past few years' appointments, are of much more immediate benefit to the people concerned with manpower policy and planning.

If the reader decides to conduct an attitude survey on his own appraisal system, we recommend that he set up *two* feedback systems at least. One system feeds information back to managers (or individual employees, or employee representatives) as soon as possible after the survey has been conducted. This enables people to get to work on local difficulties, and creates a feeling of goodwill and the impression that the survey results are being taken seriously. The second feedback system is to the central strategic planning group, who analyse the results of the survey and consider its implications for the appraisal system and the organisation as a whole. They may well decide to make changes, but these changes will take time; without the immediate feedback system people may have forgotten about the survey when the changes come through, and this affects their willingness to take part in later surveys.

Two of the most common results from such employee attitude surveys are: concern for the measures on which performance is appraised, and concern that little seems to happen as a result of the survey. Employee pressure forced at least one multinational to change from personality to performance measures, and in firms where the criteria of performance have not been well researched this pressure sometimes forces such efforts. Employees' concern that little seems to happen as a result of the appraisal is a more difficult problem; one does not usually want the appraisal interview to result in fireworks and dynamic action each and every time. But such concerns usually indicate a need to clarify responsibilities in the gathering of, and action on, training and development data.

The reader who is interested in designing an attitude survey will find advice in Oppenheim[4], and Stewart[5]. Simple surveys, that give quick and clear results, are better than long documents that have to be computer-processed; and one should not ask questions unless one knows (a) what the answers tell one, and (b) that one is prepared to take action if necessary on the matter the question refers to. Otherwise expectations will have been raised needlessly.

Surveying managers' problems

Here we give an example of a rather unusual survey, developed as a result of the need to examine why, in a particular firm, managers were not completing their appraisals on time. (Some of them were more than a year overdue.) Pressure of work, lack of support from senior managers, absence of need to appraise, were all given as excuses and some attempts made to lift their loads. Then the questionnaire which is quoted as Appendix 6.2. at the end of the chapter was developed, on the Pareto principle that if we could identify and correct the 20 per cent of the appraisals that were causing 80 per cent of the difficulties we might make a useful contribution.

The questionnaire consists of a series of opposite statements about the appraisal interview, ranging from the purely administrative to the more dynamic aspects of the meeting. The items on the questionnaire were developed by studying managers' comments about the appraisal system; different items might be more relevant to another firm. A sample of managers, of unknown appraisal record, was selected and visited. Each manager was given one copy of the questionnaire and asked to think back over the past year to the most satisfactory appraisal interview he had conducted. He was asked to describe it by ticking the appropriate boxes on the questionnaire; he was not asked to name the subordinate with whom the interview took place. After some general conversation, he was then given a second questionnaire and asked to fill it in about the least satisfactory interview he had performed during that same period. Though he was not required to name names, he was required to think of a real interview and not to regurgitate what he had heard on his last training course. Then he was asked if he had any further thoughts or concerns about the appraisal system and appraisal interviewing, and the interview drew to a conclusion.

Chi-square tests, conducted with the aid of a desk-top calculator, isolated in one afternoon those items on the questionnaire which significantly distinguished satisfactory from unsatisfactory appraisals as far as the appraising managers were concerned.

In this particular company most of the significant items concerned the appraisee's career path. When the manager thought the appraisee had come to the end of his path, or was not sure of his possible career path, then he found the interview difficult. It is fair to say that this outcome had not been foreseen at the beginning of the research, and up to this point assistance to managers in career counselling had been fairly rudimentary and not helped by the company's propensity to reorganise itself every two years or so. Training, and back-up information to managers and employees, was initiated; for example, a booklet was prepared telling employees about the work of other parts of the organisation, because most of them knew only their own patch. Managers were encouraged to tell someone when they thought his promotability was low – if these judgements are soundly arrived at, one is only confirming what the person already knows and it usually comes as a relief.

There were some surprises in the non-significant items, also. Training did not seem to have much effect. Appraising someone you have selected was less satisfactory than appraising someone you had inherited or been forced to accept. Whether or not the interview took place in the office made no difference (contrary to one of the personnel department's shibboleths). Suffice it to say that this simple questionnaire, which took managers no more than three-quarters of an hour to complete twice, and very little time to analyse, led to the identification of a number of trouble-spots and the co-ordination of action to correct those that were correctable. A questionnaire on similar lines, altered to fit the reader's own appraisal system, is likely to produce similarly useful data.

Summary

Appraisal systems need monitoring. In the early days they need checking to see how well they fit; later on they need checking to see that managers have not become blasé, and that the system still fits the real needs of the business. Several ways of checking are suggested: reviewing appraisal records for their quality, etc.; following through to see if actions suggested on the forms are in fact taken; following through predictions to see if they are borne out; attitude surveys of employees to see how they feel about the system, and attitude surveys of managers to discover where they have most difficulty in carrying out appraisal interviews. Examples of such monitoring activities are given and discussed.

Appendix 6.1 Survey of management development systems

1 Age:

Years		Years	
a. 19–21	☐	f. 41–45	☐
b. 22–25	☐	g. 46–50	☐
c. 26–30	☐	h. 51–55	☐
d. 31–35	☐	i. 56–60	☐
e. 36–40	☐	j. 61–65	☐

2 Length of service:

Years		Years	
a. 0– 5	☐	b. 6–10	☐
c. 11–15	☐	d. 16–20	☐
e. 21–25	☐	f. 26–30	☐
g. 30+	☐		

3 Length of time in present job:

Years		Years		Years	
a. 1	☐	b. 2	☐	c. 3	☐
d. 4	☐	e. 5	☐	f. 6	☐
g. 7	☐	h. 8	☐	i. 9	☐
j. 10	☐	k. 11–12	☐	l. 13–14	☐
m. 15–16	☐	n. 17–18	☐	o. 19–20	☐

Years		Years	
p. 20–25	☐	q. 26–30	☐

4 Grade:

a. 16	☐	e. 20	☐
b. 17	☐	f. 21	☐
c. 18	☐	g. 22	☐
d. 19	☐	h. 23	☐

5 Do you think that staff appraisals are:
   - a. Too frequent ☐
   - b. Frequent enough ☐
   - c. Could be more frequent ☐
   - d. Nothing like frequent enough ☐

6   The frequency of discussions with your manager, concerning your career development, is:
    a. Sufficient for you   ☐
    b. Insufficient for you   ☐

7   Indicate the type of training you feel has been most valuable during your time with the division:
    a. Internal divisional courses   ☐
    b. Group courses   ☐
    c. External courses   ☐
    d. On the job/management coaching   ☐

8   Was your attendance initiated at all the above courses by:
    a. Yourself   ☐
    b. Your manager   ☐
    c. Your manager's manager   ☐
    d. Manpower resources manager   ☐

9   What effect do you think the various staff development systems have had on your career so far?
    a. A great deal   ☐
    b. Some   ☐
    c. Little   ☐
    d. None   ☐

10   At appraisal interviews has your manager told you something about yourself that you didn't realise:
    a. Often   ☐
    b. Sometimes   ☐
    c. Infrequently   ☐
    d. Never   ☐

11   After discussion with your manager about your career development and training needs the action taken has been:
    a. Appropriate training   ☐
    b. Secondment   ☐
    c. A project   ☐
    d. Change of job   ☐
    e. Other action   ☐
    f. No action at all   ☐

12   If you have not discussed your career development with anyone other than your manager, would you welcome an opportunity of doing so?
a. Yes   ☐
b. No   ☐

13   Do you think the type of courses available internally are:
a. In need of a complete overhaul   ☐
b. Not relevant enough   ☐
c. Fairly appropriate   ☐
d. Very appropriate   ☐

14   In a well integrated staff appraisal, training and career development system, the significance of and links between the various areas of activity should be plain to see. In the case of this division is this:
a. Very obvious   ☐
b. Discernible   ☐
c. Not very apparent   ☐
d. Completely obscure   ☐

15   How long does your appraisal interview take?
a. More than 1 hour   ☐
b. 30 mins to 1 hour   ☐
c. 15 to 30 mins   ☐
d. Less than 15 mins   ☐

16   Discussions about your career development are usually initiated by:
a. You   ☐
b. Your manager   ☐

17   The situation is:
a. Satisfactory to you   ☐
b. Unsatisfactory to you   ☐

18   If you have attended any courses, indicate the frequency with which you have been briefed (briefing means advised of purpose and potential benefit of course. It does not mean told where to go and what to do) by your manager

prior to attendance:
a. Never   ☐
b. Seldom   ☐
c. Most times   ☐
d. Every time   ☐
If you have never attended a course, please tick this box
☐ e.

19   In addition to your manager, who do you think is the most
      appropriate to contribute to a fair appraisal?
      a. Your manager's manager   ☐
      b. Someone whose own work depends on
         yours being done effectively   ☐
      c. The manager of b. above   ☐
      d. Someone else   ☐

20   As a result of discussion with the manpower resources
      manager the following has taken place:
      a. Further discussion with your manager   ☐
      b. A development plan agreed   ☐
      c. A development plan implemented   ☐
      d. Nothing   ☐

21   When your appraisal interview takes place, would you say
      that it is:
      a. Not at all open and constructive   ☐
      b. Not very open and constructive   ☐
      c. Reasonably open and constructive ☐
      d. Very open and constructive   ☐

22   Do you think that some form of staff appraisal or assess-
      ment system is:
      a. Very necessary   ☐
      b. Useful but not essential   ☐
      c. Of limited value   ☐
      d. Completely useless   ☐
      e. Potentially harmful   ☐

23   Taken overall, has all of the training you have received over
      the past five years been:
      a. Very useful   ☐
      b. Useful   ☐

c. Of doubtful value   ☐
d. Not at all useful   ☐

24   Do you think that the present appraisal system has solved
     the problem of standardising ratings by different managers:
     a. Very badly   ☐
     b. Not very well   ☐
     c. Fairly well   ☐
     d. Very well   ☐

25   Discussions with your manager about your career develop-
     ment and training needs take place:
     a. More than twice per year   ☐
     b. About twice per year   ☐
     c. Once per year at appraisal interview   ☐
     d. Less than once per year   ☐

26   How frequently does your manager discuss with you your
     reaction to courses you have attended?
     a. After every course   ☐
     b. After most courses   ☐
     c. Seldom   ☐
     d. Never   ☐

27   Does the present system give
     a. Very bad   ☐
     b. Poor   ☐
     c. Fair   ☐
     d. Very good   ☐
     identification of training needs.

28   When you consider the promotions and appointments that
     have been made over the past few years, do you think that:
     a. Much useful talent has been passed over   ☐
     b. Some better system of selection would seem
        necessary   ☐
     c. The majority were well founded selections   ☐
     d. Every promotion/appointment was completely
        justified   ☐

29 Does the present appraisal system in use in the division assess performance:
   a. Badly ☐
   b. Not very well ☐
   c. Fairly well ☐
   d. Very well ☐

30 Indicate who usually identifies your training needs:
   a. Yourself ☐
   b. Your manager ☐
   c. Manpower resources manager or his staff ☐
   d. Some other party ☐

31 Is good performance rewarded by expanded promotional opportunities?
   a. It definitely is not ☐
   b. It doesn't seem to be ☐
   c. Probably, I'm not certain ☐
   d. Yes, very definitely ☐

The remaining questions (except No 39 which is for everyone) are for managers/appraisers only.

32 Does the present appraisal system create motivation to improve performance:
   a. Badly ☐
   b. Not very well ☐
   c. Fairly well ☐
   d. Very well ☐

33 Indicate which services, if any, offered by divisional training dept. you have used:
   a. Aid in identifying training needs ☐
   b. Recommendations of courses/training methods ☐
   c. Implementation of courses for your staff ☐
   d. Other services ☐
   e. None of these ☐

34 Do you regard the format of appraisal forms used in recent years as:
   a. Very relevant and useful ☐

b. Helpful to a degree ☐
c. Of little value ☐
d. Completely useless ☐

35 When do you discuss with your staff their training needs?
a. During staff appraisal only ☐
b. During staff appraisal and other times ☐
c. When training needs are identified ☐
d. Never ☐

36 Do you find appraisal interviews:
a. Easy ☐
b. Fairly easy ☐
c. Fairly difficult ☐
d. Difficult ☐

37 How would you describe the appraisal system as a management tool for improving performance?
a. Very effective ☐
b. Fairly useful ☐
c. Not much help ☐
d. Useless ☐
e. Damaging ☐

38 Would you say that to show appraisal forms to the appraisee is:
a. Quite wrong ☐
b. Questionable ☐
c. Perhaps a good idea ☐
d. Highly desirable ☐

39 What do you think of this questionnaire?
a. Interesting and relevant ☐
b. Amusing but not relevant ☐
c. A nuisance but harmless ☐
d. A complete waste of time ☐

Appendix 6.2 Managers' appraisal survey

1 It was his first appraisal   He had had one or more appraisals

2 The interview lasted more than two hours   The interview lasted two hours or less

3 I had a clear idea of his career path   I had no clear idea of his career path

4 He specifically requested an appraisal interview   The timing of the interview was controlled by the system

5 I did most of the talking   He did most of the talking

6 I told him what my own objectives were   I did not tell him what my own objectives were

7 I told him what the section's objectives were   I did not tell him what the section's objectives were

8 The job underused his skills   The job was too big for him

9 We talked about his prospects and promotability   We did not mention his prospects and promotability

10 He and I had the same idea about the direction of his career   He and I had different ideas about the direction of his career

11 I had been a manager for more than one year   I had been a manager for less than one year

12 It was the first appraisal we had had together   We had had appraisals together before this one

13 It was a male employee   It was a female employee

14 My manager agreed with   My manager disagreed with
    my rating before the   my rating before the interview
    interview

15 He wanted to be a   He wanted to be a specialist
    manager

16 The appraisal was on   The appraisal was late
    time

17 My rating came as a   My rating came as no surprise
    surprise to him   to him

18 He argued against my   He accepted my rating of him
    rating of him

19 My manager contested   My manager agreed with my
    my rating of him after the   rating of him after the
    interview   interview

20 He fitted in with the rest   He stood out in some respects
    of the work group   (not necessarily good or bad)
                                 from the rest of the work
                                 group

21 We wanted the same   We wanted different outcomes
    outcome from the   from the interview
    interview

22 He wrote on the form in   He wrote nothing on the form
    the space for his
    comments

23 My own appraisal was   My own appraisal was not
    overdue at the time   overdue at the time

24 I had received training in   I had not received training in
    appraisal procedures   appraisal procedures within
    within the previous two   the previous two years
    years

25   I had received training in appraisal skills within the previous two years   I had not received training in appraisal skills within the previous two years

26   He had worked for other firms   We were his first employer

27   He had experienced other forms of appraisal programmes   He had no experience of other forms of appraisal programmes

28   I could visualise him as my manager some day   Over my dead body!

29   My manager showed concern when reviewing the completed form   My manager showed no concern when reviewing the completed form

39   We stayed in the office for the appraisal   We went outside at some point

31   He had prepared well for the appraisal   He had not prepared for the appraisal

32   We agreed (or set) objectives   We did not agree (or set) objectives

33   I selected him for the job   I inherited him, or was forced to accept him.

Finally, how did you rate him?   _____
(and some demographic
questions)

7 Problem performers

From time to time, appraisal interviews highlight the problem of people whose performance is different from that expected. Problem performers usually fall into two types: the ones you know you have, and the one you're not sure you have. The first type are most often those whose performance is unsatisfactory: the second represent more complex problems – people in the wrong jobs, restless people, bewildered people, middle-aged people who have run out of steam. Unsatisfactory performers are brought to one's attention whether one likes it or not; the corporate ear must be closer to the ground to detect some of the other difficulties. How can the appraisal system be used to help in the management of problem performers?

Poor performers

This book is not the place to discuss the technicalities of employment law; detailed handbooks are available elsewhere. It seems a safe assumption to make though, that legislation is going to continue making it more and more difficult to dismiss people; there is a concomitantly greater tendency, on both sides of the Atlantic, for employees to institute actions for unfair dismissal. Having to fire somebody has always been a sympton of a mistake, and of missed management opportunities; now it costs more. It is a sad fact, however, that there is very little written about the management of ineffective performance; some particular problems have been worked over in depth (for example, alcoholism, social deprivation) but there are few general overviews. The advice given here is based on research and management practice, but there is need for more sharing of experience.

Why do people perform unsatisfactorily? We need to know why, because increasingly managers' options are limited to prevention and cure; like it or not we can no longer run away from the problems by firing them. People fail at their jobs when one or more of the following things are wrong:

(a) *intelligence:* insufficient verbal ability, or non-verbal

121

ability; intelligence too great for the task; specific defects of judgement or memory, etc.;

(b) *emotional stability:* over excitability, anxiety, depression, jealousy, sexual philanderings, more serious neuroses or psychotic states, alcoholism, drug addiction, etc.;

(c) *motivation to work:* low motivation, low work standards, unorganised motivation to work, strong motivation frustrated at work, conflict of motivation, etc.;

(d) *physical characteristics:* illness or handicap, inappropriate physical characteristics, lack of physical strength of endurance, effects of ageing, etc.;

(e) *family situation:* domestic crises, separation from family, social isolation from peer group, worry about money, etc.;

(f) *work groups:* fragmented work groups, over-cohesive work groups, inappropriate leadership, wrong mix of personalities in the team, etc.;

(g) *the firm:* inappropriate organisational standards, poor communication, insufficient investment and managerial support, excessive spans of managerial control, responsibility without authority, etc.;

(h) *external influences:* employment legislation, consumer legislation, safety legislation, changing social values, economic forces, changes in location, etc.

From this brief list, culled from a number of research investigations into unsatisfactory performance, we see that unsatisfactory performance is not a simple matter. A man may be performing badly because he does not want to do the work or finds himself physically or mentally incapable of it; this is the simple hypothesis that many hard-headed managers adopt. But it is very important to realise that he may be performing badly because the organisation has given him the wrong job to do – for example, the young lady with a master's degree in business administration, recruited for what she was told was a challenging position in the administration of the firm's communication system, who found herself in charge of the typing pool. She left within six weeks; nobody had told her that this job was merely a step on the way to something much greater (though we suspect that this story was invented by her ex-manager as a cover-up).

He may be performing badly because the job is no longer possible because of outside changes over which the company has no control – the arrangers of employee share-option schemes, for example, who found that they could not perform well in their jobs because the government of the day abolished such schemes. And there are occasions where someone is perceived to be performing badly because he and his manager share different views of the job to be done, or the standards to which it is to be done. The literature on innovation and creativity is littered with examples of employees whose performance was judged unsatisfactory by managers who could not recognise brilliance or who shied away from it. On a different level, middle managers are very often the first people to detect symptoms of organisational collapse; but if their own managers are incompetent and not predisposed to listen to information they don't like, then the middle managers may be judged incompetent or insubordinate.

The appraisal system provides a vehicle for examining whether there is, in fact, a difference in standards between man and manager; the appraisal interview offers opportunities to discuss whether or not the appraisee finds himself in the wrong job, and gives both parties a chance to discuss and make plans. If the appraiser's judgement of the appraisee differs greatly from the appraisee's own, then the appeals system, in whatever form, allows for a second opinion. Some managers will find this aspect of the appraisal system threatening; in discussing someone else's poor performance, they find that their own managerial practices are under scrutiny. If they would rather keep their heads in the sand, then that is their privilege, but this attitude renders other parts of their managerial anatomy excessively vulnerable.

You can use the appraisal system to fire poor performers, going through the routine of written warnings and interviews, but it is more fruitful to use the appraisal system to *manage* poor performers. How is this to be done?

Some firms have tackled the problem by management training – getting their managers together for training in dealing with poor performers, with and without the performance appraisal system. Effective training results in managers having a more realistic view of the complex causes of poor performance; a wider view of the personal and organisational remedies available to them; and a stronger motivation to manage poor performers rather than be managed by them. Training methods include group discussion, case studies, individual skill improvement by behaviour analysis and related methods, and lectures. Managers sometimes feel that their managerial prerogatives have been eroded beyond hope of recovery, and an exhortation/lecture may lift their spirits. However, training courses specifically on this topic are rare, and one does not often come across the subject on general training courses. We believe there are many opportunities here.

Managerial action on unsatisfactory performers can be broken down into four possible areas: counselling, training and development, changing the job, and termination. There is a logical order to these actions, with counselling as a first resort, and termination as a final option.

Counselling

Counselling is constructive listening and calls for skill and self-restraint on the part of the counsellor. In this respect it differs little from a good appraisal interview – the appraisee should do most of the talking, ideally coming to his own assessment of the situation and inventing his own solution; the manager serves to interject questions, making sure that options are fully examined, realistic goals are set, and so on. A good counsellor will have some notion of the problem he faces – he will have done his homework on the situation, perhaps discussing it with his own manager or with a personnel expert. He will also have prepared himself mentally for the role of listener; even if he can see the answer to the appraisee's problem clearly he must so arrange things that the appraisee thinks he thought it up for himself. Not an easy job, the role of counsellor.

It is helpful if the employee has prepared himself also, perhaps by some form of self-appraisal or preparation for counselling form. Regular use of preparation for counselling forms is one way of ensuring that problem performers are detected early, often by the appraisee himself, so that counselling action is taken before bitterness develops.

Some firms maintain special counselling functions for their employees, and opinion varies on their effectiveness. In the US, the Ford Motor Company began a counselling system in 1914, but it was considered to be too paternalistic and was eventually abandoned. Other firms maintain central counselling services and claim a fair degree of success. A small firm probably cannot afford to set aside the resources for a full-time counsellor, so that counselling must be divided between the appraising manager and any resources he can prise free from the personnel department. There are some special counselling needs that probably require professional skills:

vocational guidance, where appraiser and appraisee are in serious doubt about the appraisee's capabilities. A series of psychological tests can help establish basic abilities, trainability, and perhaps attitudes and motivation. This is particularly useful when someone is being redeployed.

mid-career guidance, for the man in middle life who suddenly experiences a crisis of identity – often called the mid-life crisis or the 'male menopause'. Redeployment or redundancy sometimes highlights this problem, which can profit, in serious cases, from professional help.

medical help, where there is a suspicion that the unsatisfactory performance is caused by, or is leading to, medical problems. Private medical screening services, such as those offered by BUPA, include questions on industrial stress in their programme, and the offer of a check-up may be the most tactful way of getting medical counselling accepted.

financial counselling, where unsatisfactory performance is due to worries over money. At the lower end of the wage scale, people get confused by the variety of benefits and deductions and might welcome help which could be given by a personnel officer or someone else with special training. Middle managers who have seen their own living standards fall drastically can be helped to stretch the money further by professional financial counselling, which a number of UK firms have been offering.

Apart from these four areas, counselling for job improvement is very much a matter for the appraising manager and the appraisee. The counsellor should be sympathetic and support-ive, but firm; he should concentrate on the work to be done, rather than on the appraisee's personal problems – in other words, not treating the appraisee as if he is a 'patient'. It some-times helps for the counsellor to tell about occasions when he himself sought help; for the appraisee to have made some mis-take is nothing to be ashamed of, as long as he knows what they have been and is prepared to try to overcome them. If the counsel-lor has the respect of the appraisee then his admission that he him-self made mistakes will help persuade the appraisee to do better.

A good counsellor learns a variety of trigger questions with which to keep the interview going: 'Why did it happen that way?', 'Would you like to tell me some more about that?' 'How long ago did all this happen?' and so on. Two questions especially useful in counselling situations are: (i) when one detects that the problem being described is somehow held at arm's length, described too generally, or with too many other people involved, to ask a question such as 'Who owns this problem?'. Often this question helps to focus on the real problem, and it certainly focuses attention on the fact that in a counselling interview you can't solve any problems other than those of the person being counselled. And (ii), when the problem has been aired in some detail, to ask 'If someone came to you with this problem, what would you advise him to do?' Even though they may recognise the trick being played, appraisees often respond better to this question than to the more direct 'And what are you going to do about it?'.

A counselling interview that focuses on unsatisfactory performance should have as one of its outcomes a list of things that the appraisee will try to do better. Such a list is often a necessary part of one's defence if employment is later terminated. It is likely to be a more constructive list, with more commitment from the appraisee, if the list contains some things that the manager will try to do better also. The more concrete these good resolutions, the better. The appraisee himself should be able to tell whether he is meeting the new targets; there should be short term, objective, observable measures for him to use, so that at the next counselling interview he can start the discussion rolling with a progress report. As far as possible the counsellor should strive to keep the number of good resolutions down to a manageable size – between three and six. And the targets should be attainable, though not without effort; the goal is improvement, after all. Improvement targets should not be set with the intention of proving the man a failure.

The reader will see that we have assumed a series of counselling interviews. The minimum is two, one to form the good resolutions and one to check progress. A common mistake, if performance improves after one counselling interview, is for the appraising manager to let matters rest. This ignores the motivational effect of sincere praise for good performance, and is reducing the likelihood of successful counselling should the employee require it again later in his career.

Managers at the end of a counselling session sometimes fall victim to a natural human tendency to claim the credit for any improvement. They can thoroughly demotivate someone who has tried hard to improve, by putting a friendly arm round his shoulder and saying 'I knew you'd feel better once you came round to my way of thinking.' A good manager gives the credit for the improvement to the subordinate.

Salary, merit awards, wage increases, and the like, should not be discussed in a counselling interview.

Training and development

Most appraisal systems ask the appraising manager to make recommendations for training as a matter of routine. In addition, training needs may become apparent during the appraisal interview or during any related counselling interview. The appraising manager may be able to delegate some of the corresponding work to a training officer, but not all. It is useful to think of training in terms of 'What do we want him to be doing differently, and by when?' and then to work out a means of achieving these ends which may or may not involve training courses.

There are many good books and articles on training, experts to be consulted, and experience to be gleaned, and we shall not discuss the design of training courses here. Small and medium sized firms are particularly well placed to use the Industry Training Boards, which provide assistance in training for firms too small to maintain a large training department. There are one or two general points to be made about using training to help manage poor performers.

First, try to make sure that particular sorts of training course are not regarded as 'punishment blocks' by employees in general. Once training has the reputation of being for punishment, or even remedial, the motivation to learn is lost.

If you use a training course, make sure that before the course the manager concerned talks to the potential trainee, enlisting his acceptance of the need for training. Ideally the training need should have been jointly identified. In the worst possible case the man gets a note on Friday afternoon telling him he's on a course next Monday.

Ask for detailed report-back on a trainee's performance only with discretion and with the trainee's knowledge. From time to time we have been guest lecturers on courses where, we have noticed, trainees behave with remarkable stiffness. Questioning this unforthcoming attitude, we have been told that at the end of the course the trainees' managers receive a report on the trainees' conduct during the course. Not surprisingly, then the trainees behave on the course with great circumspection, trying to make as few errors as possible; for they know that their managers will not understand the vital point about training courses, which is this: a training course should be an easier environment than the actual job, in which participants experiment with new ways of doing things in the knowledge that if they make a mistake, it doesn't matter. From the point of view of learning, mistakes are a vital clue to the success of a training course. But if someone feels he has to put up a perfect performance because his manager will receive a report, then he is more likely to freeze into old ways of doing things than to try new ones.

It's a good idea for a trainee to come back from a course with a plan of action that he is ready to discuss with his manager. And courses with an element of assessment are feasible, and can be very fruitful. But we would strongly advise against *secret* report-back from trainer to manager, and put the responsibility for post-course discussion firmly with the trainee.

Training courses are not always necessary. An on-the-job coaching programme, in which the manager draws up a learning plan for the poor performer and guides him through it, with or without the help of the personnel department, is a feasible alternative. Indeed, when a whole organisation suddenly discovers that it is not performing well (because the market has changed, for instance) then sensible re-training strategy may be to train supervisors in the organisation of on-the-job training. Rackham and Morgan give examples of this kind of training in airline reservation staff[1], and many other firms have similar experiences.

We have written as if training were directed towards the remedying of specific deficiencies, and in the case of poor performers, who are by definition in acute need, this may be so. However, we gave a list at the beginning of this chapter, showing factors which contribute towards poor performance; some of these factors are domestic and environmental. One pioneering UK firm, who employ a relatively small number of service engineers to maintain expensive capital equipment in customers' premises, noticed that many of their engineers were experiencing domestic and social problems which, they discovered, were due to the change in life-style that came with the large salaries they were earning – far above the UK norm for engineers. They, and their wives, found themselves mixing at a different social level from the one they were brought up at; and many of them felt exposed by not having a university degree. With great tact a personnel manager arranged with one of the older universities for a course to be given during the university's summer break, on which a wide variety of topics would be offered to a selected group of engineers and their wives. The programme had enormous success in generally broadening the trainees, easing strained marriages, and helping them catch up on things they might have missed. Many engineers whose performance was subcritically poor benefited from this most imaginative use of training courses to manage poor performance.

Changing the job

The appraisee may be performing badly because the job is wrong for him. It takes some subtlety for the appraising manager to realise this, because he probably put the man in the job himself. However, once the problem has been identified, together they can explore ways of changing the job or learning to live with the difficulties.

Some jobs are physically badly laid out, but nobody has thought to change them as they have been passed from one jobholder to another. Although the standard British lathe remains suitable for a three-foot high dwarf with a six-foot arm span, there are still some alterations that could be made to the physical configurations of the job. Older people are particularly likely to make mistakes when their work is wrongly paced – can they be given control of the pace of their work, even on a production line? Can the instrumentation be better laid out? Is the office arranged so that things needed most often are closest to hand? The appraisee can be his own work study expert, questioning why the job is arranged as it is.

Changing the timing of the work by means of flexible working hours is frequently tried nowadays, usually with great success. Reports on flexible working hours indicate that the advantages far outweigh the disadvantages for most people. The 'crime' of lateness is abolished, making the employee responsible for the management of his time within the allotted limits; if transgressions occur, the problem is at least an adult one, not bickering over five minutes here and there.

Sometimes it becomes obvious that an employee is in the wrong kind of job entirely. Usually it is a person who has been with the company for a short while only. New graduates are particularly prone to give this sort of problem. In some firms it is possible to transfer the employee from one department to another. The firm's personnel systems, and its managers' expectations, should allow for this change of mind without loss of seniority or regard. (One company expects new graduates to choose a career stream within three months of joining. After that, they cannot change. The firm loses 40 per cent of their graduates within the first year, and blames the graduates.) It may not be possible to move a bad fit into a different job entirely, but nonetheless the job can be changed by job redesign, in which the individual is given more, or different, responsibilities in addition to his present job. The intention is to arrange the job so that instead of doing little bits of a job, the employee performs a coherent task – more operations on the same unfinished product, for instance. Job redesign is a particularly effective solution when the quality of work is low, rather than the work quantity; white-collar workers respond better to job enlargement programmes than blue-collar workers. The IPM publish a useful handbook on the art of job redesign[2].

Job redesign programmes seem to have been most widely publicised at the lower end of the white-collar spectrum. Some blue-collar workers positively reject it; typical is the woman whose job filling cream cakes or sewing on suspenders takes so little of her concentration that she can day-dream in peace; ask her to add jam and sugar to the top layer, or to sew the whole garment, and the job becomes an intrusion into her fantasy world. We have not seen much job redesign at middle managerial levels either, probably because people are less sure what questions to ask. Some common managerial problems that could be helped by job redesign are:

> responsibility without authority
> no feedback on performance
> late or distorted feedback on performance
> too many 'figurehead' duties
> little or no control over the job content
> insufficient warning of changes
> shared management of subordinates.

It is difficult to give firm guidelines on job redesign because it depends much upon the problems. But it is good tactics to involve the poor performer himself in the design process, because then he has a vested interest in the success of the scheme.

Termination

The threat of termination is often thought to be a manager's prerogative, and managers of the old school regret the passing of this weapon. In fact, organisations have had to manage with very little in the way of real sanctions for a number of years; Wellington could afford to call his army scum, but Nelson had to keep on better terms with his sailors, being on the same ship for most of the time. Some of the threats may be a little emptier than they used to be, but they were never heavy with meaning.

Threats can be misused. They can be used to relieve a manager's feelings, and like an unfulfilled curse come back to their maker. They can be made in public, or brought into the open, and there made to grow for the benefit of other interested parties. Honour is then at stake, and the purposes of performance appraisal may be lost.

Threat changes behaviour when it is seen as legitimate and can be backed up. Thus many people report successful control of absenteeism by using spot checks at home by visiting nurses and other members of the personnel department. Here the stick works well when combined with a carrot – positive incentives, by means of points systems or similar devices, offered to people with a good record of attendance. On the other hand, threats are relatively ineffective in reducing accidents; accident-prone people tend to resent authority and therefore to resist safety rules. Threats connected with the enforcement of these rules are perceived as a challenge from authority. Better here to strive for group-evolved safety norms, using the techniques of hazard analysis.

Termination itself, though regrettable, need not be a rushed and graceless process. Many firms recently have had to face the prospect of firing people in grades of employment previously regarded as secure, and have learned that it is possible, once the decision to terminate has been made, to get some benefit out of it for both parties. Financial arrangements need careful attention; payments can be arranged so that, for the same outlay of the company's money, the separated employee is a great deal better off. Time off to look for a new job; vocational guidance; retraining in old skills or special training in the skills of being interviewed – all these can be offered to ease the pain of parting. And the company should not neglect the possible benefit to be gained by exit interviews conducted immediately before departure. Exit interviews

are not material for systematic study: they happen when people
are 'demob-happy' and are consequently prone to distortion, but
very occasionally at an exit interview something will be said
which reveals a severe morale problem or other area of concern.

To sum up on the management of unsatisfactory performance,
the appraisal interview offers the beginning of a process whereby
appraiser and appraisee can jointly try to manage their way out
of the problem. Though the appraisal system can also provide
the legal vehicle for warnings to unsatisfactory performers, its
major benefit is the opportunity it provides for the early detection of, and action on, poor performance.

Other problem performers

At the beginning of this chapter we indicated that problem performers came in two varieties; obvious and less obvious. The
appraisal system sometimes makes explicit the fact that there are
people unhappy with the way they are being managed, distres-
sed, or just plain bewildered. The simple research questionnaires
given in the previous chapter should help to point out any overall
trends in the difficulties that problem performers are experiencing. Some of the most common problems are:

New graduates, or similarly highly qualified people, perceiv-
ing a mis-match between their own capabilities and the jobs they
have been given to do. This is a difficult period, often lasting as
long as eighteen months, and it is often made worse by poor
induction procedures. One remedy is to use the appraisal system
for setting *induction objectives* of a kind that allow the newcomer to find his way around the business. A frequent problem
with new graduates is that they only discover the questions they
should have asked on arrival when they have, in fact, been with
the firm a few months and the implied loss of face in asking such
questions is then too great. Induction objectives (e.g. 'Draw up
the organisation chart and job description for your department,'
or 'Do an analysis of all calls coming into the department for a
week') can, when combined with frequent appraisals, help in the
painful transition from inexperience to experience.

Older employees who feel they have reached their ceiling but
are seemingly reluctant to have their feelings confirmed. This is
more often a problem with the appraising manager than with the

one appraised; the appraising manager feels that he should be in a position to offer promotion at some time in the future, and is reluctant to discuss prospects without this certainty. In fact, when a man has reached his ceiling in the organisation, for reasons that have to do with his own skill rather than internal politics or other external forces, then the likelihood is that he knows this. If he is given timely and honest confirmation by his manager (and note that we say the manager's *confirmation* of the appraisee's existing belief; the golden rule is to get his statement first), and if he has the opportunity to expand in his present job as much as he requires, then he is likely to settle down into a more contented and productive existence. With his experience he can be given special projects – looking after the suggestion scheme, monitoring current affairs or proposed legislation, liaison with the local Chamber of Trade, for example. Remember that the most accurate judge of a man's own performance, and to some extent his capacity in his present job, is the man himself.

Employees for whom there is no clear career path. The presence of this problem highlights the need for good career planning and good careers information for the appraising manager. Too often, especially in small firms, manpower planning and career planning are not done well, with the consequence that blockage can occur, blind spots arise, or fantasies multiply about the way people get promoted. Managers need back-up information about the sort of careers their people might follow, so that they can answer questions readily. And especially in firms where a large number of technical specialists are employed, there may be a need to design and promulgate a specialist career path, without large managerial responsibilities, for the sizeable number of specialists who may not want to become managers but do not see any other options open to them if they are to progress.

Employees with a sad history, the problem employees left behind by a previous manager. Every appraising manager should exercise caution when planning for the appraisal of an employee new to his team. The occasional, inevitable personality clash between a man and his manager can be recorded in the appraisal form, and it is easy for the incoming manager to take on the viewpoint of the previous appraiser. It is good discipline to build in a mental warning light that comes on whenever one reads a highly critical or highly complimentary appraisal of a new employee, in case it is necessary to adopt a different attitude.

There are other reasons why problems occur during the appraisal process. Very rarely are they actually caused by the appraisal system – unless it is a system that has been badly designed and left unmonitored. Instead, the act of reviewing performance together sometimes throws into high relief the existing difficulties. A manager may feel threatened by the appraisal process – someone is implicitly questioning his 'right', as a manager, to make judgements about his people the way he sees fit. Small but long established firms may experience a generation gap, as managers who struggled through the early days working sixteen hours a day, re-inventing the wheel, addressing their own envelopes and collecting their own debts, suddenly find themselves appraising a generation of people with entirely different standards and expectations – secretarial help, sophisticated machinery, day release, residential training courses and so on. It can be very difficult for some senior managers to accept things have changed. It is not easy to recommend solutions that will help such people, but some of the more obvious difficulties are minimised if the performance appraisal is performance-based, not based on character or personality traits.

Problems may occur when appraisal happens across sex or racial boundaries, with the added complication that one or both parties may be on the alert for unfair practices. Again, much of the answer turns on the importance of appraisal on *performance*; the *golden rule* for appraisal interviewing – 'ask him how he feels he has performed first' which will avoid heightened feelings due to the 'judgemental' role of the appraiser; and the appraiser's *consistent* practice with the timing of appraisals so as not to make the appraisee feel the odd one out. In addition, some research of our own shows that in appraisal interviews women are much more demotivated than men by early knowledge of failure. Opening the appraisal interview by reviewing the previous year's mistakes is not likely to bear fruit – in the way of later improved performance – for either sex, but in general women's performance suffers more from such news. The better practice, for both sexes, is to begin by establishing what went well, then allowing the mistakes to be put into context, preferably by the appraisee himself.

With all types of problem performers, the importance of access to a second opinion cannot be over-stressed. At the stage of preparation for the appraisal, the appraising manager should be able to talk with a disinterested outsider if he has any doubts.

In some companies this function is fulfilled by the 'grandfather' seeing, or signing off, the part of the appraisal form which the manager completes before the interview. Where 'grandfather' appraisals, or appraisals by a third party using managers' records, are performed, then the anticipatory check on poor performers happens automatically. There should also be an opportunity for disagreements during the interview to be taken to a third party, although there are signs of something seriously wrong with the system if third-party visits happen often. Here the employee may be assisted by his union representative or another good friend, if he so wishes. In some firms the employee's representative takes up the disagreement in the absence of the employee himself, but this procedure is rather cumbersome. After the appraisal interview, though, any disagreements recorded on the appraisal form should be monitored, perhaps by grandfather, perhaps by some central resource. If the appraisal forms go to the personnel department for analysis – for manpower planning, training planning, salary administration, for instance – then a trusted person can monitor the interview record and get in touch with the appraising manager if he feels there is something to be investigated further – structuring his intervention in a helpful, non-judicial fashion, of course.

Summary

The appraisal system helps manage poor performers in a number of ways. It allows for early identification of problems, by both parties, and the routine of counselling and standard-setting is a good way of overcoming problems. Unsatisfactory performers require handling in stages from counselling, through training and development, and changing the job, to termination. The appraisal system provides the records on which termination can be defended, but this provision should not be uppermost in managers' minds when conducting the appraisal. Professional help may be required with vocational, medical, or financial counselling. Problem performers may also experience difficulties through being in the wrong job, having the wrong expectations, having had poor induction training, or through having no career path visible to themselves or to their manager. The appraisal system, sensitively used, gives early warning of such problems and helps both parties manage the problem.

8 Performance appraisal systems in context

Appraisal systems do not exist in isolation. They nearly always generate data which other parts of the firm can use; our examples of central planning and control purposes for the appraisal system illustrate the many uses which a central personnel department can find for the system. It is a pity that sometimes these central purposes come to predominate over the individual motivational purposes of the appraisal interview; nonetheless many organisations have struck a balance between the interests of the parties involved, and find uses for the collected appraisal data.

In this chapter we discuss some of the more common interfaces between appraisal systems and the other planning systems: selection, induction, training, manpower planning, research, and the assessment of potential. While not attempting a complete coverage of each of these areas, we indicate the way appraisal data can be used to improve them.

Selection

Here there are three areas of impact.

1 *Performance criteria.* It was suggested in the Chapter Three that the performance criteria used in the appraisal system should be based on empirical research. If this research is done, then information about the criteria for successful performance should obviously be fed back to the selection system; there are usually some performance measures which are easier to select out than to train after engagement. Whether or not the appraisal criteria have been based on empirical research, efforts should certainly be made to see that the appraisal measures agree with the selection measures. Many cases exist of people being recruited against one set of standards only to be appraised on another set. Take for example the case of the technical salesmen who were selected by means of an aptitude test; the higher they scored the more likely they were to be hired. Unfortunately for them the salesman's job required, in practice, a *moderately* high degree of technical

ability; people who were very adept technically tended not to make good salesmen as they became too interested in the details to attend to the customer. Now we are not suggesting that there should be complete agreement between selection criteria and appraisal criteria – people will learn and grow in their jobs. But care should be taken to see that they do not get in each other's way.

2 *Questions at interview.* As more and more people come to have experience of appraisal schemes, it becomes more important to exchange experiences at the selection interview. People may have experience of a system whose purposes do not match those of the employing organisation. For example, a manager may be hired from a firm where salary is a forbidden topic at appraisal interviews into a firm where the appraisal system is used to administer salary increases. A good deal of mis-understanding will be saved if, at the selection interview, he is asked about his experience of appraisal systems and told about his new employer's. This precaution also applies to firms who grow by acquisition; they may suddenly acquire a whole new family of employees with appraisal experience different from their own. People who have had unpleasant experiences of appraisal systems in the past are particularly vulnerable here, so their past experience is always worth checking.

3 *Modifications to selection procecure.* From time to time the people responsible for selection will recruit into the organisation unsuitable people. Some of them (one hopes) will leave. Their performance appraisal records, coupled with exit interviews, may provide clues to why they were unsuitable, which the select-ion people can use. For example, in one company selling high prestige products applicants at selection interviews, gathered in groups, were given a morning-long talk about the company, stressing the quality and prestige of its products and conveying to the salesmen that they would soon be hob-nobbing with the great men of British industry. There was a deliberate effort to instil into them an almost officer-class mentality. When they finished their training and got out on territory, they found it was not like that at all; they might find themselves carrying pieces of prestige equipment up and down Oxford Street on a wet afternoon with instructions not to come back until they'd sold them. They dealt with secretaries, not bosses; they had to wait in line with other salesmen; they sometimes had to make running repairs to exist-ing equipment before they could sell any more, a procedure

which damaged their image and their best suits. Many of them left complaining that life was not what they had been told it would be. A study of performance appraisal records was the first step in an investigative programme to remedy this situation, as a result of which the recruiting procedures were substantially altered.

A performance appraisal system, in all stages of design, yields data which the selection system can use, to get a better fit between the two sets of criteria. The selection system can also modify the appraisal system, though more subtly. Here we have in mind cases where the selection officers have detected a change in ambition or motivation in the people applying for jobs, and have fed this information back so that the appraisal system can respond in time. A change in the attitude of young graduates was reported by one American company; whereas previously they had wanted to progress through the management ladder, now an increasing number wished to remain specialists. This had implications for career planning in general, and for the career counselling part of the appraisal interview.

Induction

Induction is not usually handled well. Many firms have induction programmes at the shop-floor level, or to take care of large influxes of new recruits, but the solitary newcomer, or the more senior person, is often left to fend for himself. This leads to some fairly well known phenomena; for instance because they have made so many silly mistakes in their first months they believe the record totally black; now they know what not to do, and what to ask about, they can move to a new employer with confidence. This is an expensive way of getting graduates accustomed to industry. And not only new graduates are vulnerable – married women returning to work are another large group who can get similarly lost.

For people whose job involves using their discretion, a good induction training programme should be structured so as to give them the maximum opportunity to find out for themselves about their place of work; in particular to find out the answers to silly or naive questions which they only learn to ask long after people assume they know the answer. In one or two firms this training programme is linked into the appraisal system from the first day in the job. The newcomer, on arrival, also receives an introduction to the appraisal system. This booklet describes the way the system works, its purposes, what it means for the participating employee; and it also gives a date for the first appraisal interview, which is six months from joining. (Of course, there will be informal interviews, and plenty of them, before this first formal one.) At this interview he will be expected to discuss his progress in achieving the *induction objectives* which form part of his job in the next six months. Firms using this system vary according to whether they use a pre-set list of objectives or leave part or all of the list to the manager's discretion. In any event, the induction objectives are set so that they give the newcomer a legitimate opportunity to ask questions, find things out, and settle down. Examples of induction objectives are:

> to give a report analysing the queries which come into the newcomer's department (and, perhaps, into neighbouring departments);
>
> to draw up an organisation chart and job descriptions for the people in a given sector of the firm;
>
> to draw a map or maps showing the products made, and functions carried out, at each of the firm's locations;
>
> to find out about all the training courses offered by the firm, and to interview a sample of participants to discover their views;
>
> to analyse back issues of the company newspaper and present a report showing trends, interesting issues, and so on;
>
> to compare company advertising with the competition for the last five years, and present a report showing issues for action.

Other examples will doubtless occur to the reader. The newcomer who sets out to achieve his induction objectives is guided into asking questions, and has a cast iron excuse (that he has a report to write) for asking naive questions. Induction objectives can be deliberately framed to widen the vision of people who enter with limited ambitions or restricted career paths, thus making later career management easier. And in six months' time, when the newcomer comes to his manager for the first appraisal interview, the stage is set for a more participative interview than might otherwise be the case – he has a concrete piece of work to present, he has something to talk about, and his manager's task of using the interview for counselling and motivation is greatly eased.

As we stated at the beginning of this section, induction is not usually done well, and there are few firms using induction objectives or, indeed, any planned experience during the first few months' employment. We expect the number to increase as people become more expensive and as the costs of a selection/induction mistake become relatively higher. It takes little work, and firms who do use the system report good results in terms of fewer people leaving, earlier acceptance of responsibility, and easier career management.

Training

When employees say that nothing ever seems to happen as a result of appraisal interviews – and quite a lot do say that – then they are often talking about training and development issues.

In most firms the link between training and appraisal programme is made obvious by space on the form for the manager to recommend training or developmental action during the following year. Firms vary widely in the success with which they manage the link between writing on the form and actual training. There are a number of issues to be addressed if the link is to be managed well.

1   *Why managers recommend training.* Some managers recommend their people for training because they want to have their performance improved. Others, as we have seen, use training – or particular training courses – as a punishment, or as a reward, even to use up a given allocation of training days. We once gave a seminar on industrial stress where we began, as is customary, by asking people to introduce themselves and say why they were there; one man responded 'I'm Joe Bloggs from XYZ, and I'm here because the finance course was full.' It is not always managers' fault; there is a trainer struggling at this very moment to make a training course which had achieved its objectives in eight days stretch to ten weeks because the unions had negotiated the new duration.

Managers should be encouraged to distinguish training for improvement from training for reward, if the firm insists on using training as a reward. We believe it is never right to use training as a punishment. The consequences of this for management training are discussed later in this section.

2 *How managers recommend training.* Earlier in this book a distinction was made between recommending training courses, and mentioning a specific training need. It is better if managers think in terms of training needs first and foremost; then they or the training officer can extrapolate from the needs to the required training. To think first of a training course is to limit oneself to the courses one knows, and to address the solution without first confronting the problem. Again, managers are not always to blame; many an in-house training department, or an external course-running group, responds to a client's stated needs by analysing these needs in terms of the packaged solution they have to offer.

One reason for thinking about training needs first is that a training need does not automatically imply a training course; it could be better served by a special project, or by on-the-job developmental activity. It is an encouragement to a lazy manager if he can hive off his responsibilities for on-the-job development by writing the name of a training course which someone else will provide. Another reason is that in the area of interpersonal skills, management skills, and administrative skills, people's vocabulary to describe training needs is often limited. It is easy to succumb, and write down 'communications course' or 'management training', when a little analysis, difficult though it might be, would lead to a tighter and more operational description of the training need. Technical training needs do not suffer so much from this lack of vocabulary, so that both needs and courses tend to be better defined; we are fairly happy to see technical training needs described in terms of training courses, but much less happy when we see a recommendation for 'management training' or 'budgeting.'

3 *How managers train on the job.* There has been a good deal of interest lately in *coaching* as a management skill. Coaching is really an intensified, tightly-focused version of appraisal; man and manager together identify a training need, and plan to give the man on-the-job experience which will fill the need. The progress of the experience is monitored by regular review meetings, at which they review what has been learned so far and set new objectives for the next task. The manager uses these interviews to give the man the benefit of his own experience, while making sure that the learner is as self-organised as possible. It is common to

find learning plans stretching over six months, with fortnightly review meetings in the early stages.

The manager who conducts an appraisal interview well usually does a good job as coach. Coaching as an alternative to formal training has a number of advantages: it is cheaper, it does not take people away from their work, it often has more credibility to the trainee, and the manager is helped by the discipline of having to teach. The trend towards coaching therefore gives greater emphasis, in the appraisal interview, to on-the-job training and development rather than sending people away for formal courses. At the very least this may mean some form redesign for some organisations! It also has implications for management training – coaching skills do not come naturally. Where coaching is much used, the training data collected by the personnel department will change, and the kind of follow-up activity they perform must also change. From spending their time booking people on training courses, they may change to monitoring managers' coaching activities; this is not an easy task. If much use is made of special projects or developmental assignments, then the personnel department becomes involved in extracting data about suggested projects from appraisal forms, putting the data together to decide who should go where and for how long, and negotiating swaps between managers; there may also be a role for a central person to act as counsellor, coach, and career manager to the people on assignment.

Coaching, with its immediate consequences for managers and its less immediate consequences for the appraisal system, may have a special role to play in matrix organisations also. Such organisations usually suffer from poor training; people putting together a project team choose the people best equipped, which means that chances of learning new skills are reduced unless specific plans are made to counteract this tendency. The personnel expert's role as negotiator of assignments, and monitor of on-the-job training, is crucial.

4   *How managers use training afterwards.* Many managers send their people on a training course and neglect to ask afterwards what the trainee learned, what he is going to do differently, and how the manager can help. Thus the benefits of training are dissipated as soon as people get back into the real world. Managers who use training as a punishment are often prone to crow over a returned trainee who confesses to having learned something. 'I knew you'd be reasonable and see it my way sooner

or later', they say, thus destroying most of the training's value. It is difficult to know how to overcome such attitudes, but one simple step seen on some appraisal forms is this. Before writing anything about training or development work required in the coming year, the manager must refer to the previous appraisal form and note what happened to the training needs identified then. This safeguard goes some way towards making managers aware that training is a continuous process.

Many appraisal training programmes give managers no guidance in identifying training needs. Filling in the form correctly, and interviewing skilfully, are well served; but training in identification of training needs, counselling, drawing up developmental plans, etc., is sadly lacking. We shall return to this need later in this chapter, when we discuss the assessment of managerial potential. Management training programmes should possibly pay more attention to getting managers thinking about training needs and analysing performance in detail. One simple exercise for use in such training involves giving groups of trainees a transcript of a conversation – a committee meeting, a negotiating group, or the like – and asking them to study the characters taking part and draw up a list of their training needs. This usually brings out for discussion matters like the influence of the observer on what is observed; the need for specificity and objectivity when describing training needs; and the need to collect evidence in a balanced fashion.

One firm took the problem of getting managers to identify training needs so seriously that it organised a series of short seminars for managers and training officers. Two of the high spots were: an exercise in which managers drew up a list of the things they wanted from their training officers, while training officers drew up a list of things they wanted from their managers, after which the two lists were compared; and an exercise in which group of managers were provided with a pile of training brochures and a telephone, and told to find a training course to fit a real, identified training need which one of the managers had. The first exercise was useful in pointing out the cracks, before and after training, where manager and trainer hand over to each other. And the second gave insight into the problems of training needs diagnosis, especially as it was practised by the course-runners whom they telephoned.

Manpower planning

There is often a direct link between the appraisal system and the manpower planning system. Indeed, in some firms this link is so strong that line managers believe the appraisal system exists to enable the personnel department to do better manpower planning. While this should not be the case at all, it is foolish to ignore the planning activities that can benefit from appraisal data.

Good books on manpower planning are beginning to be available, though in essence the subject remains one for specialists. A good overview can be obtained from Bartholomew[1], Morris [2], and the books they recommend. Here we can only outline some of the uses to which appraisal data are put in manpower planning systems.

1 *Simple forecasting*, by for example taking present data and extrapolating to discover what the position will be in x years' time if nothing else changes. Age data are often used here, and potential problems picked out in time for remedial action to take place: bulges of people approaching retirement, say, or gaps in certain age groups. Other measures beside age may be used – education, for example, or experience with the firm, or performance on the appraisal criteria. Using these more subtle measures predictions can be made about career blockages, for instance, in time for preventive measures to be introduced.

2 *Succession planning.* If the appraisal system asks managers to record opinions of the employees' potential, perhaps with data about employee preferences, then simple succession plans can be drawn up, covering each job more than once and making sure that people are trained well in advance of jobs for which they are identified.

3 *Internal labour markets.* Companies of any size who wish to maintain some flexibility amongst their employees – they might want to transfer employees from one location to another, or from one job to another – find that their internal labour market is not usually as fluid as they would like it to be. The appraisal system can be used to collect data about career preferences, mobility, domestic situations, etc., which give the firm a better view of its internal labour market. With a little more help from experienced manpower planning experts it is possible to go on to make predictions about what will happen to the market. One common example of such a prediction concerns the wastage rate.

Companies wishing to reduce manpower by natural wastage are sometimes tempted into extrapolating from their present wastage rate, not realising that their present wastage rate contains a large number of leavers who have been with the firm for only a short time; the longer people stay with the firm, the less likely they are to leave. Putting a ban on recruitment ensures that the work force becomes composed of long stayers. Also, as people realise that jobs are not being filled their behaviour changes; some will choose to hang on to their jobs, when they might previously have been mobile. Others, usually the best workers, leave for other jobs while the going is relatively good and they have some choice left. These and other factors make prediction by simple extrapolation useless; but with the application of existing manpower models to the appraisal data better predictions can be arrived at.

4   *Costing benefits schemes.* The appraisal data may be useful for costing certain benefits schemes. Pensions commitments, to take a simple example, can be costed by an examination of the present age structure, together with modifying factors such as the rate of employee turnover in each age group. When legislation on sex discrimination came into force many financial institutions who offered cheap mortgages to their male employees found it necessary to consult the records to discover how much it would cost them to extend the benefits to female employees. Other benefits, where there is likely to be selective take-up or differential usage, need costing with the help of simple data from the appraisal scheme.

As manpower planning becomes more sophisticated the uses that appraisal data can be put to will multiply. Already systems exist for storing 'soft', qualitative data without falling into the trap of spurious precision, and these systems enable predictions and plans to be made with more subtlety. Though sophisticated statistics, and computers, are needed centrally for the manpower planners to do their work, systems are available which allow the amateur to get information using plain language. With this increased power, and with the high cost of manpower and the even higher cost of manpower mistakes, it is saddening to realise that there are major UK organisations who have only the haziest idea of how many people they employ, and to whom the idea of collecting more sophisticated information for planning purposes has never, it seems, occurred.

Research

Appraisal data make a good hunting ground for the personnel researcher. We have already mentioned some of the research projects: constructing a talent drain index, for instance, to compare appraisal ratings of those who leave with those who stay; or going through old appraisal forms to discover the kinds of objectives managers actually set during appraisal interviews. If the researcher has permission to look through the records, there is almost no end to the issues he could examine. Some further examples of research amongst appraisal records are:

1 *Identifying trouble spots*, where it is suspected that a particular product, or type of customer, or geographical location, is giving problems of a sub-critical level. Examination of appraisal records may show one type over-represented as a cause of problems, in which case further investigation is called for.
2 *Examining equity*, where it is required to see if one group of employees is receiving more favourable treatment than another group. Most often this is done between the employees of different managers in the same function, so that people doing comparable jobs are compared with one another. More unusual, but often more profitable, is to compare employees in different functions; one firm doing this discovered that specialist and professional employees were being passed over for career movement, compared with other groups, because their managers thought they were tied to particular projects for a long time and were therefore immobile. In another firm in the same industry precisely the opposite was found; managers of specialists were over-fond of putting their people forward, because they perceived a lack of places available to them. In both cases analysis of the appraisal records played a major part in the discovery.
3 *Examining morale*, when the part of the appraisal form that is left for employees' comments (if it is present on the form concerned) is examined. Trends in what employees say – with whatever evaluative connotation – are noted and judgements made about morale in general and any particular problems that may be highlighted.
4 *Examining managers' judgements*. It is often instructive to look at the performance measures managers are supposed to use, and to compare how they actually do use them. For example, if there is a five-point scale, are managers using the full five points

(or four points if the bottom one is supposed to be for unsatisfactory performers)? If they do not use the whole scale, how well are they discriminating between people? Do they want to make such judgements? Are the scales meaningful to them, or should they be changed for others? A scale that is not used to make discriminations with is not a useful scale, and should perhaps be dropped. Similar questions can be asked of the way managers set objectives: are they clear? could another manager use them? are they relevant to the job being done? These and other questions can be asked if, for example, managers' training needs are being looked at.

5 *Detecting deviations*. If an employee has been a consistent B performer, and his performance suddenly drops to D, then it may be worth investigation. Many personnel departments operate a system whereby automatic warning is given of any sudden change in an employee's performance, so that gentle investigation can be started. There may be a change of manager, who brings different standards to the job; there may be sudden domestic or health difficulties. A check to see whether the manager has the matter in hand, and perhaps an offer of independent counselling, follows the identification of the deviation.

6 *Inducting strangers*. For obvious reasons this is not a common research activity, but there may be times when a stranger needs to get to know the organisation fast – a company doctor, for example. To make the appraisal records available to such a person, with the names obliterated perhaps, is a quick way of giving him a feeling for the organisation and its problems. It is high-risk, and must not be mismanaged, but if it works it works well.

And all this research can be conducted without leaving the ivory tower in which the records are stored! The reader will no doubt think of many other ways in which appraisal records can be used to investigate wider problems within the organisation. From time to time research is done on the actual appraisal interview, by having an observer in the corner while the interview takes place. He might be monitoring such things as: the balance of conversation in the interview; the manager's use of questions; the proportion of time spent on each issue; the appraisee's frequency of agreement or disagreement, and so on. Research by Terry Morgan of the Air Transport and Travel Industry Training Board, and others, has shown the kinds of behaviour from both parties which make successful, and unsuccessful, appraisal interviews. However, in-house research that involves sitting in on the actual interview may be fraught with danger; it must be very difficult to have an ordinary appraisal interview with one's boss when there is a silent observer from the personnel department sitting in the corner. Outsiders are probably seen to be more trustworthy, though this cannot be guaranteed. Live research on the interview as it progresses *must* be subject to the same degree of reliability checking as ivory-tower research; just as the researcher going through forms to classify them should get someone to do an independent classification from time to time, so the person who sits in on an appraisal interview taking notes about the proceedings should also check his reliability by cross-checking with another observer. Otherwise one will unconsciously bias the results towards observing only those things which confirm one's hypothesis.

Identification of potential

Many appraisal forms require the manager to make a judgement of the employee's potential. Usually this is on some simple scale showing where he is expected to be in a given number of years, or how many years it will take him to reach a given grade. This system is fraught with danger, and the reader will have gathered already that we have strong reservations about using the performance appraisal system as a measure of potential. We have expressed these reservations, along with our suggested solutions, in a book on the identification of management potential, *Tomorrow's Men Today*[3]. Briefly, some reasons why the appraisal system should not be used for assessment of potential – or at least should not be the exclusive measure of potential – are as follows:

1   *Simplicity of the measure.* The measurement of potential on a simple scale, as most companies do, is so simplistic as to be unreal. It implies only one direction of growth, with uniform distance between the steps, whereas in real life there are many different career directions and many different contributions a man may make.

2   *Confidence in the measure.* When the Institute of Manpower Studies conducted a survey into company practices in the assess-

ment of potential, we were often told that managers lacked confidence in the judgements of potential they were making. This lack of confidence was particularly apparent when we suggested that judgements of potential be made known to the employees themselves. We were disturbed to find that out of all the companies we surveyed, only one company using the appraisal system for predicting potential gave managers any training in making these predictions, and that training consisted of a half-hour talk in the half-day's appraisal training for managers. The rest made their judgements untrained; no wonder some of them lacked confidence.

3 *The manager's horizon.* There is a good deal of evidence to show that when managers use track record alone as the basis of their judgements they are not good at assessing the potential of employees to reach a position higher than the one the manager himself holds. This makes intuitive sense to most people; yet many managers are asked on their appraisal form to make a judgement of the appraisee's ultimate potential, or to make judgements relating to one or two grades higher than the appraising manager's. The manager is, in effect, making judgement about the appraisee's ability to fill a job of which the manager has no personal experience, basing his judgements on the appraisee's performance in a job far removed from the one under question.

4 *Discontinuities in the system.* Most people have had experience of the good salesman, promoted because of his sales skills into sales manager, who becomes a poor sales manager. Performance in a non-managerial job is not usually a predictor of performance in a managerial job; indeed, good performance as a non-manager might disqualify one from the management job if promotions were made rationally (as many specialists and professional employees know to their cost). The discontinuity, and the unreliability of track record as a predictor, is fairly well known at the non-manager/manager transition point. There is another discontinuity at the very top of the tree, where the transition must be made from functional responsibility to board responsibility; where a finance man may find himself involved in, and taking Cabinet-type responsibility for, decisions to do with personnel, marketing or production issues. Research into the identification of management potential at this level shows quite clearly that in most firms this discontinuity exists, and is a big one. And in many firms there is a third place where track record is not a good predictor of future performance – at the middle

management level where many of the moves are a combination of the lateral and the vertical. If performance in the present job is taken as a prediction of performance in the next job, and so on, then the organisation will continue to make many promotion mistakes around these discontinuities. Sometimes they attempt to avoid this trap by asking the appraising manager to make judgements of the man's abilities whether or not they are required by the present job, but this is not usually well done.

5 *Poor performers in the wrong job.* One organisation has a rule forbidding managers to pass on poor performers to other managers; they also assess potential by reference to record in present job. When, as sometimes happens, an employee of theirs is performing badly because he is in the wrong job, there is no way for that employee except out. A number of their employees have had highly successful careers with the competition, who are not so rigid. If someone finds himself in the wrong job, it may be a while before he realises it; especially if he is young and inexperienced, or if the firm has a sophisticated-looking selection system. The manager who put him in that job has every reason, conscious and unconscious, for not recognising it. It is difficult to perform well in a job that's too small, especially when one does not know what the trouble is. The final result, after the selection mistake that started it, is to conclude that the man's poor performance in his present job implies that he has no potential for filling a bigger job As firms experience slow-downs, with consequent cuts in recruiting, and as unemployment grows so that people are more prepared to take jobs they would not have considered previously, more people are likely to find themselves in ill-fitting jobs. If with the best will in the world they cannot turn in a good performance, their position should not be made worse by assessing their potential on their track record.

6 *No job experience for appraisee.* Though the selection interview is probably the single most unreliable weapon in the personnel manager's armoury, it is still used for selecting people; and one of the reasons for perpetuating this wasteful practice, we are told, is that the interview gives the job applicant an opportunity to experience the firm, to ask questions, to see where he will be working and to meet some people doing the actual job. Now when we consider the assessment of potential of existing employees, using their track record, we discover that the track-record method offers no means whereby appraisees can experience the job for which they are being assessed to see

whether they like it. This is not unimportant; many non-managers have little idea of the real work a manager does, especially if their own manager is at all skilful. When career counselling middle-aged managers we often hear the cry: 'I went for management because there didn't seem to be anything else, there was only one way to go if you wanted promotion'. The younger generation are demanding specialist career paths, job-sharing, more personal mobility; and in any case it makes little sense to put a man into a strange job which he comes to dislike.

So, what are the alternatives, and what part can performance appraisal play in predicting potential? Of the many alternative ways of assessing potential, three seem to be common:

1   *Psychological tests* of ability, personality, motivation, etc. Research into tests as predictors of management success is constantly going on, and it can be summarised briefly by saying that while there is no universal test of management ability (and probably never will be), a psychologist may well be able to recommend tests for the particular purposes of one firm. Like any other single measure, a test will not do the complete job of prediction; and a psychological test cannot be bought off-the-peg. It must follow a diagnostic exercise of some sort to determine what factors the test should be looking for, and it must be carefully installed with concurrent and predictive validity measures taken. Besides their use as a selection/prediction device, tests are often used for career counselling. Here the data are revealed to the employee for him to make his own assessment, and counselling is structured around his results and his ambitions. For counselling purposes we recommend the interested reader to examine Stephen Fineman's three questionnaires, which examine issue of employee motivation and organisation culture, and which are given in Fineman[4]. They are simple tests which yield much useful information.

2   *Special projects.* Here a project or projects is identified as requiring a certain range of skills, and the appraisee – of whom it is required to know whether he possesses these skills – is given the project to perform. His performance is monitored, on the criterion measures, and from this limited work sample a judgement is made about his ability to perform the whole job. Examples of simple projects include the delegation by a manager to one of his subordinates of his managerial role while the manager is on holiday, or the assignment of an employee to a

particular task force or working party. The key point is the monitoring of performance – it is not enough just to give him the project; special arrangements must be made for performance to be regularly measured, preferably by more than one monitor, and preferably also by the man himself.

3 *Assessment programmes*, in which a group of employees go through a series of tasks under the eyes of trained observers. The tasks are arranged so as to simulate the job for which potential is assessed, and to bring out in participants the skills required. Tasks vary from programme to programme, but might include: in-basket exercises, leaderless group discussions, structured group discussions, listening exercises, book reviews, presentations, negotiation exercises, brain-storming exercises, essays and psychological tests. Trained observers, usually line managers, make records of the participants' performance in such a way that no observer has a monopoly of any participant and on most exercises all observers have a contribution to make about each participant. At the end of the exercise the observers meet to agree assessments of, and development plans for, each participant; and feedback and counselling interviews with the participants follow.

Each of these three methods – and there are many others – has advantages over the use of track record. In the latter two particularly the developmental impact on the person assessed is enormous; many organisations for whom we designed assessment programmes have changed the name to development programme, while not removing the assessive element. Measurements are made of the man doing the job, rather than extrapolations from his present, somewhat unrelated job. This addresses the problem of the poor performer in the wrong job, as well as giving the assessee a feeling for the job to be done.

Employee opinions about the three methods above vary. In general assessment programmes are judged as fair and open by most employees; special projects also, though by a less strong majority; and opinions divide sharply about the use of psychological tests, with one school of thought reacting with abhorrence to the notion of measurement and another school believing such precision to be a sign of the employer's competence. Most surveys into the assessment by track record system show that employees distrust its fairness (see Williams[5]). The business measures associated with the methods above appear to favour assessment programmes: several research reports (e.g. Stewart and Stewart[6] and Barnett[7]) claim that assessment programmes reduce promotion mistakes to negligible figures. The superiority of assessment programmes may be an artefact of their being rather better-researched than other methods; national networks now exist for the co-ordination of psychological test data, for instance, so we can expect more information on this method before long.

Firms who install another system for assessing potential find themselves faced with the criterion problem; what, precisely, should they be looking for in potential managers? The superiority of other methods over track record is sometimes due to the work on criteria which precedes the installation of a new system. As assessment programme designed to the wrong criteria enables one to be precisely and expensively wrong, whereas track record assessments do not invite the same attention. Sometimes, though, research on criteria has been started with a view to designing an assessment programme, or putting in psychological tests, only for the decision to be made after seeing the criteria that an adjustment to the appraisal system is all that is required. Work on assessment of potential begins with decisions about criteria, and progresses to methods next.

If a firm is to be successful using track record to assess potential then some or all of the following conditions must apply. It must be a homogeneous firm, in all directions; no sudden increases in responsibility, and no sudden changes of skill as one moves from job to job; and no sudden changes in the business climate either. They must be in a buyer's market for staff, yet hard-headed enough to fire their mistakes rather than create special jobs for them. They must have a high level of employee trust in the assessment system. Managers should receive training in the assessment of potential. Wherever possible, assessments of a person's potential should be collected on a number of criteria, from a number of observers, who have observed the man in a variety of jobs and positions. Predictions about potential should be checked, in exactly the same way as one would check predictions from a psychological test, and the results fed back to the predictors. And care should be taken to see that managers' political concerns do not influence their judgements of their own or other people's potential.

Having said all that, we are certain that no organisation should rely on performance appraisal for assessing potential without first collecting evidence to see whether this is the best way of doing it. The automatic assumption, which so many firms make, that on page 4 of the form the untrained manager can make a simplistic judgement about how far the appraisee will progress, through other jobs unfamiliar to the manager, is an assumption which needs checking and re-checking. The appraisal system has too much power to make it a vehicle for organised guess-work.

Summary

The appraisal system interacts with other systems in the organisation. The selection process and the appraisal system should be in harmony. Induction difficulties may be aided by the use of induction objectives. Training planning follows almost automatically from most appraisal systems, but managers need training to get their judgements right. Manpower planning activities, in all their forms, use appraisal data; and in-house research may use appraisal records for a variety of purposes. The use of the appraisal system for the assessment of potential is fraught with danger, and other assessment methods should be considered before settling for track record as a basis for prediction.

9 Relations with outside bodies

A number of outside bodies have an interest in the appraisal system, and in some cases their role can be crucial. During the planning and the maintenance of the appraisal system the trade unions or staff associations and the Industry Training Boards can be uniquely helpful. During the time the system is running it may be called into question by bodies who administer the employment law of this country. In the nature of things, there are no strict immovable guidelines to these bodies' points of view; however, some general advice may be helpful to enable the reader to get the best out of them.

Trade unions and staff associations

Most national trade unions show little formal interest in appraisal systems as such, being more interested in improving pay and working conditions for their members. This may change as more professional and managerial people become unionised, and the vagaries of pay policy sometimes force people to take an interest in appraisal systems when they would rather concentrate on collective bargaining.

Where there is a union or staff association, the staff representative should be brought into the discussions on the appraisal system as soon as possible. There is in this book a clear separation between decisions on the *purposes* of the system, and actual system design; we advise wide consultation about the purposes of the system, while the system design is left to experts. The committee designing the appraisal form without a clear statement of purposes will not automatically become better if a staff representative is included. So we suggest that staff representatives be consulted about the purposes of the system; that they be encouraged to discover what their members think about the idea of appraisal; and that their ideas be listened to constructively. It is not unknown to find that the staff representatives take a much more individual, motivational approach to the idea of appraisal; that they value the discussions and counselling above the more mechanistic aspects of the system.

Staff representatives can usefully be involved in the familiarisation and training that happens when a system is installed. They should certainly be present during familiarisation and commitment-getting meetings; preferably speaking about the system rather than being told about it. It is tempting to involve staff representatives by asking them to explain the grievance procedure, or by giving them a similar 'us-and-them' role; better, if the preparation has allowed it, to ask them to talk about the motivational side, or about the way the performance criteria are to be applied.

It is when the system is installed and running that most firms are vulnerable to trouble from the staff association. When standards slip and things are allowed to get slack, they may notice earlier than the personnel department. This is one reason why we laid stress on the need constantly to check and maintain the system, and perhaps to do specific pieces of research into the system. Without such watchfulness the system could degenerate into a sophisticated annual punishment ritual, or into a complex form of salary administration. Besides the intrinsic problems this brings, such a degeneration will lead in turn to difficulty in negotiating about the system when its difficulties become apparent; people will have acquired different views about its purposes over the years but may not be able to articulate them.

If you monitor appraisal returns by counting simple numbers, or if you classify forms by their content and monitor any changes, then the staff representative should perhaps be able to see the figures too – though people's anonymity should also be protected. If you have a system for flagging when one person's appraisal rating suddenly takes a tumble, then the staff representative may be better equipped than someone from the personnel department to discover whether there are special problems that need help. If you are planning a survey to examine people's attitudes to the appraisal system, then the staff representative may have some questions to suggest. He can perhaps help analyse the results; he can stand guarantor of the anonymity of the answers, if you want this. He can help with interpretation, with feedback, with implementing any suggested changes.

These suggestions assume a basic honesty on the part of the reader and the managers in his organisation. They assume a willingness to take responsibility for conducting appraisal interviews sensitively. If, despite all the opportunities to be participative and open-minded, managers want to use the system for grading people, deciding how much to pay them, and telling them when they are out of line, then at least the staff representative should know that this is what the system is being used for; don't pretend that it is the latest technique for improving human relations. Also, openness with staff representatives implies that managers should not be asked to make judgements which they cannot defend. We found a number of managers who said that if they had to defend their secret rating of an employee's potential to his face then they would not make it. If the staff representative is to see that rating, then it should be made with confidence or not at all – which means not at all for many of the judgements managers are asked to make.

Some firms involve their staff representatives even more deeply. They may be called on in the event of a grievance resulting from the appraisal interview, to accompany the appraisee in a visit to grandfather or the personnel department; in some cases the appraisee may even request the presence of a staff representative during the appraisal interview itself. If this becomes a regular practice then there is a danger of the appraisal process becoming tainted with too much flavour of discipline, but when it is used sparingly employees often feel better in the knowledge that the safeguard exists.

There has been a good deal of talk lately about industrial democracy; usually this has materialised as discussions of forms and formulae – who is to sit on what board, how, and with what responsibilities. There is another form of industrial democracy, in which all parties are brought closer together by shared aims, informal communications, trust and mutual respect for expertise. We suggest that staff representatives be involved in planning, conducting, and day-to-day running of the appraisal system, so that the spirit of industrial democracy becomes an inextricable part of the appraisal system.

Industry Training Boards

Most British industries are covered by an Industry Training Board, who are there to advise on training and related activities such as appraisal systems and management development. The impetus from the training boards has in many cases resulted in appraisal systems being installed where none existed before;

some used the power of the levy-grant system to ensure that satisfactory appraisal systems were put in.

Individual boards vary in their interest in appraisal systems; some, like the Chemical and Allied Products ITB, have done a great deal of research into appraisal, while others have hardly looked at it. In general, though, the ITBs' expertise falls into the following areas:

1 *Specifying purposes* for the appraisal system. They can help in the early stages of system design, when so many people become entangled in the details of form design and forget to look at the overall purposes for the appraisal system. An ITB adviser can, by skilful questioning, bring the subject back to the basic question: what kind of intervention into your firm do you want to make with your appraisal system? As an outsider he can bully people gently to make sure that their understanding of their purposes is full and complete, and he can help the decision process by giving examples of appraisal systems in other firms. Some ITBs have a very high level of expertise on this question, and their advice can be invaluable.

2 *Helping with form design*, after the purposes have been agreed. This may be nothing more than showing a variety of appraisal forms to let people see the available range, or it could be more detailed involvement in the actual design. Many of the practical hints on form design – the order of the items, 'the amount of space given to each question, and the layout of scales, for example – come best from someone with previous experience of design work. Also, an expert outsider's view is valuable when the form is being proof-read; the in-house designers are certain to have become blind to its faults by the time the final document is ready.

3 *Helping with supporting literature.* Appraisers and appraisees need information about the system, and this is usually provided in a booklet specially written for the purpose. Anyone with experience of writing such booklets, like the ITB advisor, helps prevent the re-invention of the wheel. He may also help prevent the wholesale pirating of some other firm's booklet, which has been tried when people are in a hurry. A good advisor has had experience of the kinds of questions people ask, and the things that concern them. He will also act as a check to make sure that the booklet is written primarily for appraisers and appraisees, and not for the personnel department; it is tempting

to describe the system in terms that make it seem personnel's baby, whereas the benefits to the line need stressing all the time.

4 *Help in commitment-getting.* We stated earlier that the presence of a prestige outsider could be useful in getting managers' commitment to the appraisal process; he legitimises the innovation, and can answer questions about other firm's experience in this area. Some ITB staff are very good at taking the role of prestige outsider, and as their experience is with related industries their credibility is likely to be high. Advisers who specialise in this role develop expertise in persuading people, and may have useful advice on aspects such as whereabouts in the room to position likely objectors. Their role in giving reassurance to managers who are feeling reluctant to embark on such an innovation is very important; they may even be able to bring along to the commitment meeting managers from other firms who have had appraisal systems installed and are benefiting from them.

5 *Help in training.* Two functions for the ITB are possible here. One is straightforward help with the design of training courses; appraisal training is not easy to do well, very easy to do badly, and has little in common with other forms of training. Trainers who have some experience in interpersonal skills training may be able to design their own training programmes, but trainers whose experience has been confined to technical training, or to knowledge-giving courses, may find design troublesome. Some training boards have a high standard of expertise in appraisal training and will give direct help with design, and maybe running, of the courses. The second way in which ITBs help with training is training the senior staff. There are some firms where senior managers think it beneath their dignity to attend training courses anyway, and refuse to attend training put on by their own training staff. (One of us once participated in appraisal interview training for senior managers, at which real appraisal interviews with subordinates were to be conducted. A senior manager confessed himself surprised to find that they and the subordinates were booked into the same hotel.) Whether or not these feelings are rational they are certainly strong, and it may pay to ask the ITB, or some other outside expert, to undertake training for the senior managers.

Industry Training Boards sometimes help with the interfaces between the appraisal system and other systems – with personnel records, training planning, management development activities, and so on. It must be said that the standards of boards vary a great deal; some are centres of genuine expertise, while others cause us (and their companies) a good deal of concern. Our description of the role of an ITB must therefore be taken as an idealised statement, rather than one drawn from real life, and it does not represent a prescription of the ITBs' functions. The reader may be lucky, or very unlucky, with the help he gets from his own ITB.

The same comments and cautions apply to external consultants. There are consultants who will play all the roles we have ascribed to the ITBs here, and play them well – persuading, cajoling, and advising the people who design the system, and helping them with training and public relations. We are less happy with consultants who market a ready-prepared appraisal programme, perhaps complete with paperwork; we have so often seen these packages go sadly awry. There is a particular fondness for the packaged MbO programme, which usually works well when installed into simple sales or production divisions but causes problems in service divisions, non-profit-making functions, matrix organisations, etc. The consultant's package often brings with it a secondary problem; that people are reluctant to alter the system, once they find it doesn't quite fit, because they bought it from a prestige outsider. The more expensive the system, the less likely it is to be tinkered with, because this is seen as an admission that the original purchase was mistaken, and people cannot bear to have things for which they have suffered devalued. So, the package bought from a consultant may save time and thought in the first place, but it is unlikely to be sensitively managed once installed.

Consultant help with training is similarly variable. There are excellent courses, usually in-house, designed by consultants; and there are dreadful ones. We caution the reader against external courses where there is a mix of familiarisation with the idea of appraisal, and training in appraisal skills. The topics do not mix well, and are addressed to different audiences. Similarly courses where anyone from personnel director to office supervisor is admitted are unlikely to lead to anything useful. There is merit in mixing different levels, and different firms, but it needs more careful management than most public courses give. Our caution against mixing knowledge and skills on a public course is, to some extent, based on follow-up work on these courses; it is not uncommon to find people expressing satisfaction with the course but showing no behaviour change afterwards. The safest mix of knowledge and skills on a public course is to concentrate on the knowledge-giving and to have a demonstration interview, or even a film, to show what goes on in appraisal – but the demonstration interview is for demonstration only, and should not be regarded as training in skills.

Consultant help with monitoring the system is not often available, but a good consultant will seek to leave behind him the skills used in doing the actual monitoring; thus the firm's own staff will be involved in the research project, and be able to carry on themselves afterwards.

Legal and quasi-legal bodies

Employment law in the UK and elsewhere is becoming more and more concerned with protection of employment, and with giving employees who feel they have been unfairly discriminated against an opportunity to seek redress. There are implications here for the performance appraisal system on a number of counts.

First, the criteria of performance. They should be fair and relevant to real effectiveness in the job; and their fairness and relevance should be easy to explain. We have already stressed this point a number of times, but it will bear repeating. The same argument also applies to criteria against which potential is assessed. If this is not the case, then someone who has been passed over for promotion may call into question the criteria in an attempt to prove that they are unfair. At the moment unfairness may only be alleged – in the UK – by people believing themselves to have been passed over on grounds of race or sex; in the United States age is also a factor, and it may become one over here.

Secondly, the possibility that legal scrutiny may be brought to bear on the appraisal system has implications for the way equity between appraisers is maintained, especially if salary matters are in question. If one manager's standards can be shown to be different from another's, to the detriment of one of his subordinates, then the subordinate may wish to call this treatment amounting to constructive dismissal.

Thirdly, and most important, is the way the appraisal system is applied across employees. It is not unknown for long-running

appraisal systems to fall partly into disuse; perhaps the only
people who receive interviews are the high-flyers and the poor
performers. It has happened that someone dismissed for poor
performance has alleged that the appraisal system was being
used only in his case, and that it was therefore unfair and was not
being used as the vehicle for constructive warnings and improvement planning which the firm alleged it was. This is an easy trap
to fall into. If an employee is to be dismissed for poor performance, one should be able to show the record of warnings received. If, besides these warnings, there is a record of the plans
both parties have made to overcome the deficiencies, then the
employer's case is stronger. Many managers are quick to apprec-
iate the value of this aspect of the appraisal system, while
ignoring – or leaving until tomorrow – the motivational and
counselling aspects. Thus the appraisal system is used most carefully when poor performers are under scrutiny, but less so when
middling and good performers are concerned. We worry when
we see appraisal systems in which the manager is only obliged to
give the employee an interview if his performance is unsatisfactory; besides opening up the appraisal system to accusations of
unfairness, it ignores the massive motivational effects which the
interview can have on the good and medium performers.
Similarly we dislike systems where star performers are given
special treatment during the appraisal process.

The main problem, when considering the impact of legislation
on appraisal systems, is that appraisal systems are organic
things. Without this knowledge it is easy for the untrained outsider to believe that the system exists for salary administration
and manpower planning, just because those are the only parts
that are visible on paper. It takes skill to explain to such an outsider that the appraisal system is a vehicle for improving communication between man and manager. The outsider may pay
more attention to deviations in the concrete aspects of the
system, like the paperwork, or the frequency of appraisals, and
be less able to question the more subtle aspects of the system. In
an atmosphere where legislation is brought in to ensure good
industrial practice, it can be very difficult to convey the true
meaning of the appraisal system; even the most empirical set of
performance criteria might not stand up against someone who
wanted to make debating points. So, in the face of legal pressures
on the appraisal system, it is important to ensure that people
conform both to the spirit and to the letter of the appraisal

process, and that they understand the differences between the two; for it is better to avoid trouble in this area than to try to fight even with right on one's side.

Summary

Trade unions, staff associations, Industry Training Boards, and legal bodies may all have an influence on the appraisal system for good or ill. Where trade unions and staff associations exist, they should be involved with the planning, execution, and maintenance of the appraisal system, at as local a level as possible. They can help with many aspects of the system, not just grievance-handling, and in many cases they do it well. Industry Training Boards provide advice and expertise on the design of systems and forms, the design and running of training, and the gaining of managers' commitment. Their position as privileged and experienced outsiders allows them to make a unique contribution. Legal bodies, concerned with administering the laws on unfair dismissal, unfair discrimination, etc., act as a safety-net and provide some minimum standards, but it is not wise to get into arguments about dynamic, interpersonal processes like appraisal systems as attention is more likely to be focused on the mechanical aspects of the system.

10 Speculations on the future

The pattern of business and industry is changing rapidly; products, markets, personnel, and constraints, have altered in the past few years more quickly, and in other directions, than many people would have predicted. In this chapter we speculate about some of the changes we may see, in the UK, Europe, and the USA, over the next few years. Our reason for doing so is to indicate the implications for appraisal systems, so that readers designing a new system may not suddenly find it out of date.

Public scrutiny of performance criteria

Already, as indicated elsewhere in this book, the criteria on which performance is assessed may be challenged if someone feels that they have been used to discriminate unfairly on grounds of race or sex. Criteria such as personal appearance, friendliness, physical strength, have already been called into question. We drew a distinction between *personality* characteristics and *performance* characteristics when discussing criteria of performance, and – in company with most writers on appraisal – advised that performance characteristics were better because they were easier to measure, more susceptible to objective measurement, and gave people a better chance of improvement. But it is not the case that any collection of performance characteristics will do; they should be clearly related to success in the job. For example, one or two firms try to assess people's *resistance to stress* as a measure of performance on which they are appraised. It is an appealing measure, with the hard-nosed, James Bond image that attracts some people; but in the firms we have in mind empirical research has shown that stress-resistance (by which they mean resistance to short term overload) is not related to success in the job. If that criterion is called into question by someone who believes it to have been wrongly applied, then the firm will have a hard time defending it.

At the moment, performance criteria come under scrutiny only if someone claims unfair discrimination on the grounds of race or sex. It is easy to see how these grounds could be enlarged, either by legislation or at local levels, so that anyone could bring a case if he thought a decision was unfair. It is unlikely that a cast iron defence could be constructed by referring to empirical research on performance criteria, but such a defence would at least be much more solid than one based on 'accepted management practice' or some other committee decision. As always, the good manager will have done his homework anyway; it is necessary for job improvement to take place that people be appraised on criteria of performance relevant to that job, so that good managers will do the empirical work for business reasons. Our own, and other people's, work on installation of good performance criteria shows that the business improvements well repay the effort.

Open record systems

Some companies in Europe and the USA have allowed employees free access to all information kept about them, for many years previously. The chairman of IBM in the USA, Frank Cary, gave an interesting interview[1] in which his company's liberal position on open records was made plain.

There are two main implications for the appraisal system. One is that if the system is to be used for motivation and self-development, then the employee must see the record of his past performance. Without a chance to see and discuss it he cannot sensibly plan to improve, nor tell when he has improved. Most firms in the UK recognise this and allow the backward-looking part of the form to be shown.

The second implication concerns the assessment of potential. If this is made by a simple judgement on a straight-line scale, showing readiness for promotion in time, then the employee seeing this is likely to regard it as a promise of a job. He may also introduce it into the appraisal interview as a topic to be bargained over. Managers who feel unhappy about making predictions about people's ultimate potential may refuse if they have to defend them. All of which is an argument for doing the sensible thing: do not judge potential by reference to track record alone, unless you have good reasons for knowing this is valid; and do not condense the judgement of potential into a single measure on a single scale. Multi-trait, multi-method, and multi-observer assessments are the ideal to aim at, and it is our experience and that of a large number of firms that revealing such judgements of potential to the employee does not lead to his inferring the promise of a job.

There are other implications of open record systems. On an open record system no manager would be foolish enough to make the judgement that someone has 'no potential'. And open record systems throw into relief the problems of paying people for potential rather than for performance. They also force consideration of who shall have access to employee appraisal records, and with whose permission – a question that needs addressing in any appraisal system, but sometimes goes unanswered.

Open record systems sometimes lead to re-examination of performance criteria, or to the attacking of performance criteria in appraisal interviews. Thus the importance of having criteria based on good research, and of making sure that everyone concerned knows how they were arrived at, is again stressed.

When employees see everything that is written about them in the appraisal records they may confuse plans with promises. An assessment of potential is an assessment of the employee's potential irrespective of the job market in the future. An identified training need in a certain area is not a promise that a course will be arranged. It is important to make this clear, so that everyone concerned knows the difference between plans (probable) and promises (certain); and that they know when the employee is being compared against the job description, when he is being compared with other employees, and when he is being compared with himself; and when these comparisons are modified by external considerations.

Again, these are things that the good manager would ensure anyway, and the good employer has nothing to fear from open record systems; for the poor ones, someone may care to supply appraisal forms printed on edible paper.

Self-appraisal

Self-appraisal is in some ways a logical counterpart to open record systems, and many firms already use it; either by giving employees a preparation for counselling or preparation for appraisal form, or by giving them a facsimile of the manager's appraisal form. As more firms come to realise the motivational and developmental aspects of appraisal, the use of self-appraisal forms is bound to grow. Such forms are a very important factor in getting dialogue going in the appraisal interview, with the employee taking the lead, and they help reduce many managers' fears of being put into a judgemental role. While we ourselves feel happier with the self-appraisal form that is *not* the same as the manager's form, firms using the manager's form for the appraisee say that often the appraisee's rating of his performance is slightly lower than the manager's which gives a boost to both parties.

There are other reasons why self-appraisal is growing. One is the move towards on-the-job training and self-development, where people have to take responsibility for their own performance and for performance improvement. The self-organised learner has to be able to monitor his own performance accurately. And as appraisal becomes a serious subject amongst middle managers it becomes apparent that some aspects of a manager's performance are not easily visible to his manager, so it is better if he assesses them himself. The same argument applies to people who work unsupervised, or whose job is so specialised that the manager cannot really appraise it all. Self-appraisal for developmental purposes may be the only sensible way for these people.

In firms where there is matrix management, self-appraisal is useful. Where groups of people share responsibility for a task, self-appraisal may be a more acceptable way of isolating the individual's contribution to the task, and easier for the individual to do than for the manager. Where Management by Objectives has been tried and failed, self-appraisal systems prove a refreshing change; they are obviously not part of the downward-chaining sequence of MbO, and they make it clear that appraisals can start anywhere in the organisation, not just from the top. Indeed, wherever there has been an unhappy previous experience with performance appraisal – especially where there has been too much paperwork, or the system was used for punishment only – self-appraisal systems are a refreshing change, and may be the only way to get performance appraisal started again.

Professional career paths

We suspect that there is an increasing tendency among professional and specialist staff to demand their own professional

career path separate from the management ladder. Some professionals in industry regard the management job as a positive step
down: 'I'm a good graphic design artist, so why would I stop
doing that and take a job as a second-rate admin. clerk?' as one
such professional put it to us. There are some firms to whom this
comes as a severe shock; for them, the provision of a career path
other than through management is unthinkable. And there are
many managers of specialists, in their own middle-age, who
remember the pangs with which they gave up their work as
specialists to move into management and resent the younger
generation's demand for professional career paths.

Whether or not professional career paths are justified, and
how they should be designed and managed, is a matter largely
outside the scope of this book. (See Lansbury[2] and Stewart and
Stewart[3] for fuller discussion on this subject.) Because a group
of specialists demand one is no intrinsic reason for designing a
career path, and there is bound to be difficulty in getting one that
corresponds to the management ladder at all its various stages.
And career paths for professionals may have in them discontinuities which management paths do not; the requirement for certain types of professional skill may suddenly diminish, or the
professionals themselves may become obsolescent (really, or in
their own view) before their fortieth birthday. The size of the
problem, and the variety of professionals involved, must dictate
the overall solution. However, the implications for the appraisal
system are clear.

1 *Managers must know* the details of professional career paths
so that they can do sensitive career counselling. It is not uncommon, in medium and large firms, to find managers who have little
idea of career opportunities outside their own patch. The careers
advice they give, and the career progressions they arrange, must
necessarily be limited. Information about careers in other parts
of the firm should be provided; and in complex cases the personnel department may supply experts to assist with the counselling.
2 *Employees must know* that professional *and* managerial
career paths exist, and be given as much information as possible
about the criteria governing progress along each path. Help in
choosing may also be necessary; early experience of the work
requirements in various divisions and occupational groups helps
prevent people from becoming stuck in one career path without
seriously considering all the alternatives.

3   *Managers must be trained* not to resent it if young specialists, by turning down the management path, appear to be disparaging their own choice as managers. Some managers still have the 'If it was good enough for me then it's good enough for him' attitude, and take it as a personal insult when their protégé rejects the career path they have chosen for him.

4   *Career counselling* should, perhaps, be just what it says; counselling about the specialist's whole career, not just his career with the firm currently employing him. There is a strong tendency in some occupations for people to be mobile between employers: the computer industry, management consulting, and personnel work are all good examples of this. It costs little extra effort, if people are going to experience career counselling anyway, to arrange for them to be counselled about their whole career; and the benefits in terms of goodwill are enormous. There are other firms who still do their manpower planning on the assumption that people will join them at age eighteen and stay until retirement; they are completely unprepared for the increase in mobility of their professional staff which, we predict, they will soon be experiencing.

With more emphasis on professional, rather than managerial, career paths the type of counselling offered in the appraisal interview will change; so, of course, will the manager's recommendations for development and training and the way he assesses employee potential. The manager will have to give more thought to what the employee wants to do, rather than assuming he has only one set of aspirations which it is up to the manager to fulfil.

Mid-career change and retraining

Two or three trends meet here. The past few years have seen some emphasis on a phenomenon popularly called the 'male menopause', in which forty- to fifty-year-old men go through a period of change, turmoil, and disillusionment similar to that which women have known. We suspect that the phenomenon has always occurred; it is a combination of changed life-style when the children grow up, a realisation that not all one's ambitions will be fulfilled, a slowing-down of growth in salary and promotion rate, and maybe intimations of mortality as one realises one is not a twenty-five-year-old any more. The recent interest has partly been fuelled by the way middle managers have suffered, in comparison with the rest of the working population, during recent periods of pay restraint. Financial problems combine with personal problems in an unbearable burden; or existing personal problems receive financial expression.

Coupled with the tendency to recognise a male menopause is the need for many people to re-train in middle age, either completely or in part. This need is becoming apparent at all levels of job. There are several implications for appraisal systems here.

1 *Special counselling* may be offered to managers in mid-career who need to re-think their directions. This re-think could be prompted by their own personal needs, or by the needs of the company who see that in a few years' time there will be no need for the job presently being occupied and would like to re-train its present occupant. It is unlikely that such counselling could be done by the appraising manager; a specialist from the personnel department, or even an outside counsellor, could be brought in. Managers however need to be alerted, to see the signs of such counselling needs to be aware how the needs can be met.

2 *Career planning* will have to take account of career patterns very different from the gentle-flowing forward of the last generation. Predictions of long term potential will be useless if the managerial needs ten years hence cannot be specified, for example. Training and development needs may include re-training and re-development needs; in this case the managers who use training as a punishment will find themselves unable to recycle their people-resources, and the managers who use training as a reward will find very puzzled subordinates returning from courses where they have had to do some work. Training, in fact, will mean training, and it may hurt. The appraisal system may need support before it can be used to diagnose training needs, if these are re-training needs; managers might not diagnose new needs as well as familiar ones. and there may be a return to formal courses and instruction, away from on-the-job coaching, which managers might find disturbing.

3 *Career obsolescence* could affect some people. Now, some people believe they are obsolescent at thirty, though they have years of productive life in front of them. Others do not recognise their own obsolescence in the face of all the evidence, like the manufacturer of lock-gate equipment who kept increasing his market share until he went broke. And others are rendered obsoles-

cent by the bad planning of their own organisation, where people did not look far enough ahead. Fear of obsolescence usually strikes in specialists and professionals, though not exclusively; they are often helped by openness about performance criteria, and especially those performance criteria which emphasise the *facilitating* effect of the more senior members of staff. Self-appraisal systems help make these feelings explicit; they also help convince the people who really are obsolescent of the fact. However, the real message for the appraisal system is in the *monitoring* of the system; it needs checking to see that the system is still fulfilling valid business purposes, that it is being used smoothly and that no useful opportunities are missed, and that the performance criteria, guidance on training needs, etc., are still relevant to the problems of today and the future. Old appraisal systems are dangerous unless controlled.

Pressures to bureaucratise

The increase in the amount of legislation to be complied with, and the records that must be kept and rendered up when called for, has for many firms meant a massive growth in non-productive functions and a tendency to deal with matters by set procedures rather than by improvisation. Thus an organisation which might naturally fall into a matrix, or into an informal person-centred culture, is pressured into forming hierarchies, with job descriptions, fixed responsibilities, terms of reference, and other procedural devices. We shall not discuss here whether this hampers the effectiveness of the firm; we wish merely to point out one implication for appraisal systems of creeping bureaucracy inside an organisation. It is this: that in a truly bureaucratic organisation, it is more important that everyone perform to the same standard than that some people excel. Now one way in which appraisal systems can be used, and we believe it to be the most important use, is to motivate individual people to improve their performance. All our advice about self-appraisal, and training managers to listen, and letting people know how they are rated, is based on the assumption that people like learning and want to improve. In a bureaucracy, once someone has got himself up to the standard of everyone else, there is no incentive to improve and there may even be disincentive; people have been fined for being too clever. This tendency can be seen in some of our classic

bureaucracies; people are not given regular feedback on their performance, people are only told if they fail, people are only given
the reasons for failure. Much more emphasis is given to correct-
ing failure than to improving on success. We suggest that this is
not the right way for most entrepreneurial firms; it is not even the
right way for most bureaucracies, but the door to a bureaucrat's
mind is closed from the inside. When looking at the appraisal
system in the long term, it is useful to consider whether one really
has an organisation where success is rewarded and individual
effort recognised; and when pressures to bureaucratise are
exerted, be aware that the appraisal system may be one of the
casualties.

Trends to smaller units

We are told that small is beautiful, and that large organisations
are unwieldy and slow to react. Many big firms are trying to split
into smaller ones, and small firms are crying that they are the salt
of the earth. What are the implications of this trend for appraisal
systems?

Here is the test for the reader who believes that appraisal is
primarily a man-manager process; for if it *is*, then the size of the
firm makes no difference to the final outcome. This is why we
stressed earlier in the book that appraisal systems are for small
firms just as much as for big firms; for the motivational effects of
appraisal happen irrespective of size. If the system is the personnel department's idea, imposed on managers from a great height
in head office, then breaking the company up into small units will
scare the system's keepers because they will see their prerogatives
threatened and their nice neat systems in danger of being broken
up; but if the system is a tool for line managers to manage better
with, generating useful data for the personnel department on the
side, then the worry will be much less.

In a small unit records may be kept locally, not centrally, and
kept in a box rather than on the computer. This is almost certainly desirable. Manpower planning and other activities can be
carried out with very small data bases using simple computing
equipment; no need for sophisticated systems to manage the day-
to-day business of appraisal. The problems arise when the small
units are taken together – transfers are to be arranged between
two units, perhaps, or a company-wide salary scheme is to be

imposed irrespective of local autonomy. Then consideration must be given to performance criteria and rating scales: are the same criteria used over different units? do they have the same labels but used in different ways? do people have the same career chances in one unit as in another? Uniformity should be imposed only when there are very good reasons for it, since local variations often are there for good reasons. Uniformity should certainly not be imposed just to make the personnel department's job easier; someone there should be mature enough to tolerate the kinds of ambiguity that line managers have to live with every day.

Criteria other than business efficiency

With over half the UK domestic product being spent by the government and with the trend away from manufacturing industry to other ways of creating and spending wealth, more and more appraisal schemes will use performance criteria that are not directly related to business efficiency. In a number of organisations – local government, for example – personnel specialists are not sure where to get guidance on performance criteria, even when their empirical research has been done; this is much less likely to happen in productive industry, where lines of responsibility are clear up to the board and the shareholders and the other interested parties. Personnel specialists in these dilemmas will not be helped by looking at the kinds of objectives that industry sets, for industrial objectives may not be appropriate; the provision of employment may be more important than the efficient use of human resources, for instance. A nationalised industry like the railways may have to place social objectives above business objectives, and run loss-making services (or services which appear loss-making under the rather idiosyncratic costing methods used). Richard Marsh, when chairman of British Railways, was often heard to say publicly that he could run the railway to any given set of objectives, if only the government of the day would make up its mind about the objectives it wanted BR to pursue. Examples of criteria other than efficiency can be multiplied; the appointment of people by racial, political, or nationality mix rather than by ability; the siting of offices where they will bring employment rather than where they will enable efficient running of the business; budgeting which allows notional deficits to be maintained, or written off, in ways which financial probity would forbid in a commercial organisation.

We do not want to condemn these practices out of hand; some of them, and some of the organisations using them, are very necessary. We do make a plea for honesty in the management of these performance criteria; if the reader works for such an organisation, then he should recognise that some of his performance criteria will be different from the ones he will find in a merchant bank or an oil company. He should not ignore these and limit himself to commercial-looking criteria; his picture will be incomplete. And it is an interesting exercise to try to quantify such criteria, not necessarily in hard, numerical terms, but to get some sort of rating scale established. Also it is important to strike a balance between these different kinds of performance criteria.

We write as if there are two kinds of organisations; hard, commercial ones, and flabby ones spending taxpayers' money. Of course these stereotypes are not true, and more and more commercial organisations are coming to realise the importance of 'social' objectives; thus one finds them educating schoolchildren, seconding their good managers to charitable institutions, keeping employment going when economic sense would suggest making redundancies. Where this happens, the appropriate changes should be made to performance criteria or job objectives.

Treating people as investments

This is, perhaps, the most optimistic of our suggested trends. The recent changes in employment legislation, the increased hidden costs of employing people, and the use of electronic equipment to perform what the Americans charmingly call 'Mickey Mouse' work – all these considerations are forcing organisations to look on the hiring of people with the same concern and attention to detail that they have in the past given to capital investment. The importance of good selection and training is, at last, being recognised. Manpower planning and career planning activities are seen as a positive contribution to the welfare and well-being of everyone in employment, so that people continue to grow and develop and organisations share in the benefits. In some firms performance appraisal systems are being dusted down and given a new lease of life – the paper exercise foisted on them by the personnel department is suddenly perceived as a genuine management tool. Over the years that we have been concerned with appraisal systems we have noticed a change in emphasis, from discipline, control, and record-keeping, towards development, self-development, and growth. Long may this trend continue.

References

Chapter 1

1   C.N. Handy, *Understanding Organisations*, Pelican Books, Harmondsworth 1977.

Chapter 2

1   K. Knight, *Matrix Management: A cross-functional approach to organisation*, Gower Press, Farnborough 1977.

Chapter 3

1   M.R. Williams, *Performance Appraisal in Management*, Heinemann, London 1971.
2   J.F. Campbell, M.D. Dunnette, E.E. Lawler and K.E. Weick, *Managerial Behaviour, Performance, and Effectiveness*, McGraw-Hill, New York 1970.
3   D. Gill, B. Ungerson and M. Thakur, *Performance Appraisal in Perspective*, Institute of Personnel Management, London 1973.
4   A. Hunt, *Managerial Attitudes and Practices towards Women at Work,* HMSO Publications, London 1975.
5   A. Stewart, *Content Analysis: A Review*, Institute of Manpower Studies, Brighton 1977.
6   D. Webb et al., *Unobtrusive Measures: Nonreactive Research in the Social Sciences*, Rand McNally, New York 1967.
7   N. Rackham and T. Morgan, *Behaviour Analysis in Training*, McGraw-Hill, Maidenhead, England 1977.
8   G.A. Kelly, *The Psychology of Personal Constructs*, W.W. Norton, New York 1955.
9   A. Stewart and V. Stewart, *Tomorrow's Men Today*, Institute of Personnel Management, London 1976.

Chapter 6

1 C. Margerison, 'Turning the Annual Appraisal System Upside Down', *Industrial Training International*, February 1976.
2 A. Stewart and V. Stewart, *Tomorrow's Men Today*, Institute of Personnel Management, London 1976.
3 M.R. Williams, *Performance Appraisal in Management*, Heinemann, London 1971.
4 N. Oppenheim, *Questionnaire Design and Attitude Measurement*, Heinemann, London 1966.
5 V. Stewart, *How to Conduct your own Employee Attitude Survey*, Institute of Manpower Studies, Brighton 1974.

Chapter 7

1 N. Rackham and T. Morgan, *Behaviour Analysis in Training*, McGraw-Hill, Maidenhead, England 1977.
2 K. Carby, *Job Redesign in Practice*, Institute of Personnel Management, London 1976.

Chapter 8

1 D. Bartholomew, *Manpower Planning*, Pelican Books, Harmondsworth 1976.
2 B. Morris, *Recruitment, Promotion, and Career Management*, Institute of Manpower Studies, Brighton 1974.
3 A. Stewart and V. Stewart, *Tomorrow's Men Today*, Institute of Personnel Management, London 1976.
4 S. Fineman, 'A Modification of the Ghieselli Self-Description Inventory for the measurement of need for achievement amongst managers', *International Review of Applied Psychology*, vol. 25, no. 1, 1973; 'The Work Preference Questionnaire: a measure of managerial need for achievement', *Journal of Occupational Psychology*, vol. 48, 1975, pp. 11-32; 'The influence of perceived job climate on the relationship between managerial achievement, motivation and performance', *Journal of Occupational Psychology*, vol. 48, 1975, pp. 113-24.

178

5 M.R. Williams, *Performance Appraisal in Management*, Heinemann, London 1971.

6 Stewart and Stewart, op. cit.

7 G.G. Barnett, 'Identifying Managerial Potential for Long-Range Planning', *Long Range Planning*, October 1975.

Chapter 10

1 F. Cary, 'IBM's Guidelines to Employee Privacy', interview in *Harvard Business Review*, September-October 1976.

2 R. Lansbury, 'Work Attitudes and Career Orientations Among Management Specialists', *Journal of Management Studies*, February 1976.

3 A. Stewart and V. Stewart, *Professionals and Specialists: Management and Self-Management*, McGraw-Hill, Maidenhead, England, forthcoming.

Bibliography

Argenti, M., *Corporate Collapse*, McGraw-Hill, Maidenhead, England 1976.

Barnett, G.G., 'Identifying Managerial Potential for Long-Range Planning', *Long Range Planning*, October 1975.

Bartholomew, D., *Manpower Planning*, Pelican Books, Harmondsworth 1976.

Campbell, J.F., Dunnette, M.D., Lawler, E.E., and Weick, K.E., *Managerial Behaviour, Performance, and Effectiveness*, McGraw-Hill, New York 1970.

Carby, K., *Job Redesign in Practice*, Institute of Personnel Management, London 1976.

Cary, F., 'IBM's Guidelines to Employee Privacy', interview in *Harvard Business Review*, September-October 1976.

Fineman, S., 'A Modification of the Ghiselli Self-Description Inventory for the measurement of need for achievement amongst managers', *International Review of Applied Psychology*, vol. 25, no. 1, 1973.

Fineman, S., 'The Work Preference Questionnaire: a measure of managerial need for achievement', *Journal of Occupational Psychology*, vol. 48, 1975.

Fineman, S., 'The influence of perceived job climate on the relationship between managerial achievement, motivation and performance', *Journal of Occupational Psychology*, vol. 48, 1975.

Gill, D., Ungerson, B., and Thakur, M., *Performance Appraisal in Perspective*, Institute of Personnel Management, London 1973.

Handy, C.N. *Understanding Organisations*. Pelican Books, Harmondsworth 1977.

Hunt, A. *Managerial Attitudes and Practices towards Women at Work*. HMSO Publications, London 1975.

Kelly, G.A., *The Psychology of Personal Constructs*, W.W. Norton, New York 1955.

Knight, K., *Matrix Management: A cross-functional approach to organisation*, Gower Press, Farnborough 1977.

Lansbury, R., 'Work Attitudes and Career Orientations Among

Management Specialists', *Journal of Management Studies*, February 1976.

Margerison, C., 'Turning the Annual Appraisal System Upside Down', *Industrial Training International*, February 1976.

Morris, B., *Recruitment, Promotion and Career Management*, Institute of Manpower Studies, Brighton 1974.

Oppenheim, N., *Questionnaire Design and Attitude Measurement*, Heinemann, London 1966.

Peter, L.J., and Hull, R., *The Peter Principle*, Pan Books, London 1970.

Rackham, N., and Morgan, T., *Behaviour Analysis in Training*, McGraw-Hill, Maidenhead, England 1977.

Stewart, A., *Content Analysis: A Review*, Institute of Manpower Studies, Brighton 1977.

Stewart, A., and Stewart V., 'Reviewing Appraisal Training', *Industrial Training International*, April 1974.

Stewart, A., and Stewart, V., *Tomorrow's Men Today*, Institute of Personnel Management, London 1976.

Stewart, A., and Stewart V., *Professionals and Specialists: Management and Self-Management*, McGraw-Hill, Maidenhead, England, forthcoming.

Stewart, V., *How to Conduct your own Employee Attitude Survey*, Institute of Manpower Studies, Brighton 1974.

Webb, D. et al., *Unobtrusive Measures: Nonreactive Research in the Social Sciences*, Rand McNally, New York 1967.

Williams, M.R., *Performance Appraisal in Management*, Heinemann, London 1971.

Index

'A–Z Retailing Company Ltd, The' 16–21

Appraisal interview: conduct of 1–3, 93–4; grievance procedure 63, 71, 135; mention of salary increase 67, 68; records 10, (*see also* Open record systems)

Appraisal interview training: knowledge 82–5; skills 85–96: by live appraisal of real tasks 90–2, by real-life counselling 88–9, by role-play 85–8

Appraisal systems design 60–78: appraisee's purposes 61, 64–5; appraiser's purposes 61–2, 65–8; central planning and control purposes 62–3, 68–71; purposes of outside parties 63–4, 71–3

Appraisal systems, history of 12, 13

Assessment programmes 152

Barnet, G. G. 153
Bartholomew, D. 144
British Airways 13

Campbell, J. P. 37
Career counselling 2, 7, 64, 109–10, 133, 169, 170
'Cloud, Cuckoo & Partners' 21–5
Colbert, M. 13

Commitment meetings 80–2, 159

Computerised record systems 30, 105

Consultants 160

Content analysis technique 41–3

Critical incident technique 40–1

Fineman, S. 151
Ford Motor Company 124

Gill, D. 37
'Grandfather' role in appraisal 8, 9, 35, 63, 67, 135

Handy, C. N. 1
'Hardware International' 30–3
Hunt, A. 38

Induction objectives 100, 132, 138–40
Industrial tribunals 8, 161–3
Industry Training Boards 12, 63–4, 71–2, 95, 127, 157–61
Institute of Manpower Studies 104, 148
Institute of Personnel Management 130
International Business Machines (IBM) 13, 165

Knight, K. 26

Lansbury, R. 168

Management by Objectives (MbO) 5, 6, 52–3, 57–8, 65, 103, 160
Manpower planning 7, 36, 68–9, 144–6
Matrix organisations 26, 142
Mid-career change and crisis 125, 132–3, 169–71
Minnesota Mining and Manufacturing (3M) 13
'Money Brothers' 26–8, 102
Monitoring the system 97–110: checking appraisal action 103–4; checking appraisal prediction 104–6; surveying employee attitudes 106–8; surveying managers' problems 108–10
Moorby, E. 103
Morgan, T. 42, 128, 147
Morris, B. 144

Narrative summaries 55
New graduates 130, 132

Objectives 5, 6, 17, 31, 52–5, 65, 70, 98, 103, 173–4
Open record systems 11, 72, 165–6
Oppenheim, N. 108

Performance questionnaire technique 43–50
Peter, L. J. 1
Philips 13
Poor performers 99, 121–32, 150: counselling 124–7; dismissal 131–2; job

redesign 129–30; training 127–9
Potential assessment 63, 69, 148–54
Preparation for Counselling form (or Preparation for Appraisal form) 10, 31, 61, 64, 66, 75–7
Professional and specialist employees 101, 167–9
Psychological tests 105, 151

Rackham, N. 42, 128
Rating scales, design of 55–7; examples 23, 56
'Red Tape' 28–30
Repertory Grid technique 50

Salary planning 6, 69
Selection 136–8
Self-appraisal 101, 166
Stewart, A. 41, 50, 105, 153, 168
Stewart, V. 50, 105, 108, 153, 168
Succession planning see Manpower planning

Talent drain index 106, 146
Trade unions and staff associations 155–7
Training and development needs 63, 67, 60, 102, 127–8, 140–3

Webb, D. 41
Williams, M. R. 37, 106

Xerox Corporation 13